CUB SCOUT SKILLS BOOK

CUB SCOUT SKILLS BOOK

By

JEAN BARROW

Illustrated by

DAVID ANSTEY

Publication approved by The Scout Association, London

GLASGOW
BROWN, SON & FERGUSON, LIMITED
4–10 DARNLEY STREET

First Edition   *1984*

ISBN 0 85174 477 X

© 1984   BROWN, SON & FERGUSON, LTD, GLASGOW, G41 2SD
Printed and Made in Great Britain

INTRODUCTION

So, you are now a Cub Scout.

Welcome—there is a great deal of fun and laughter in store for you. You will play games, go on expeditions, cook on open fires, sing songs around a real camp fire, make new friends and learn many new and exciting things.

You are about to start on the Arrow trail—Bronze, Silver and then Gold. There are nearly 100 Arrow activities to choose from, far too many to put them all into this book. You will need to complete twelve activities for each of the Arrows, probably working for the Bronze while you are eight years old, the Silver during your ninth year and the Gold during your last year in the Pack.

Akela will introduce many of the Arrow activities into the Pack Meetings, and then the activities you are particularly interested in you will be able to follow up at home.

When you eventually become a Sixer, you will also become a Member of your Pack's Sixer's Council and will be able to help Akela to plan and maybe even to run a Pack Meeting with another Sixer.

Good luck and have lots of fun with your Pack.

MY NAME IS _____

I BELONG TO THE _____ PACK

I WAS INVESTED AS A CUB SCOUT ON _____

I GAINED THE BRONZE ARROW ON _____

I GAINED THE SILVER ARROW ON _____

I GAINED THE GOLD ARROW ON_____

MY AKELA IS _____

TELEPHONE NUMBER_____

CONTENTS

YOU ARE NOW A CUB SCOUT AND ONE OF THE WORLDWIDE BROTHERHOOD OF SCOUTS

These are the words Akela said to you during your Investiture. You are now wearing the *World Badge*. It is called the World Badge because many Scouts in countries all over the world wear the same badge. We always wear it on the left side of our uniform, over our heart. Part of our badge is the Arrowhead which shows the north on a map or compass. Baden-Powell told us that it is the badge of the Scout because it points in the right direction. The three points will remind you of the three main parts of your Promise. The Arrowhead is surrounded by a white rope in a circle and tied in a reef knot at the bottom. This symbolises the unity of world brotherhood throughout the Movement. No matter how hard you pull a reef knot, you cannot undo it, so the Scout Movement remains united. Neil Armstrong, the first man on the moon and a former Scout, took the World Badge with him on that memorable journey. Cubs in countries all over the world are wearing a uniform especially designed for use in their country, but all are Members of the worldwide brotherhood of Scouting. Wear your uniform proudly, and always respect it.

The Cub Scout Cap is a good protection from the sun or rain, and should never be used as a ball or kicked about your Headquarters.

The Scarf. Each Scout Group has a special scarf. This shows people which Pack you belong to when you are at a District Event, so always keep your scarf clean and ironed. Your scarf should be rolled, not folded and ironed flat. If you find this difficult, try rolling your scarf with the aid of a stick. The length of your scarf from point to tip should be no more than 15 cm (roughly the span of your hand).

Uses for your Scarf. To protect your neck from the sun; bandages in an emergency; as an emergency rope; a quick and easy way for Akela to spot you at a District or County Rally! Your scarf should NEVER be used as a blindfold during Pack games.

Shorts are especially ideal for summer Pack Meetings. It is much easier to scrub knees than washing and patching long trousers. Shorts give greater freedom of movement.

Garter Tabs should be worn neatly on the outsides of your socks.

Finally, don't forget to wear your *Scout Lapel Badge* on your anorak or school blazer. On holiday in this country or abroad watch out for the tiny lapel badge, and also for the larger Scout badge or Scout symbol. Many cars carry the sticker. You may even see a sticker in windows of houses.

BADGES AS EARNED AND WORN BY A CUB SCOUT

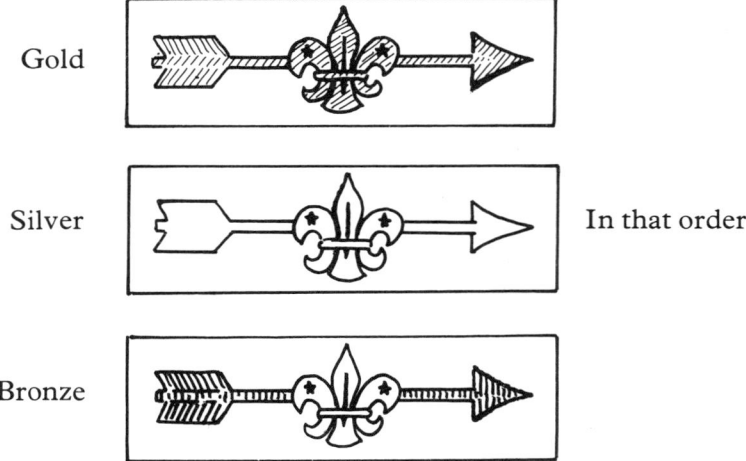

Gold

Silver   In that order

Bronze

Remember that all Cubs wear the same uniform, so it is very important to have your name on everything.

Things to Do

DISTRICT BADGE
● Why does your badge have that particular design? Find out all you can about it.

COUNTY BADGE
● What does yours show? Can you find out what it all means?

NAME TAPE
● What is your Group number? Do you know how many Groups there are in your District, and can you pinpoint their Headquarters on a map of your District?

Are you interested in swopping badges? Join the Badgers Club—Secretary: Ruth Elliott, 34 Pagets Road, Bishop Cleeve, Cheltenham, GLOUCESTER GL52 4AJ, enclosing a stamped-addressed envelope.

WHAT SCOUTERS DO

Akela and the rest of the Scouters in your Pack are all voluntary helpers. This means that they do not get paid for the hours of planning and running the Pack Meetings, the expeditions and the summer camp which all of us enjoy so much.

Scouters, too, make a Promise which is slightly different from your own:

> On my honour,
> I promise that I will do my best
> to do my duty to God and to the Queen,
> To help other people
> And to keep the Scout Law.

Perhaps you have seen one of the Scouters being invested.

Just as you achieve the Bronze, Silver and Gold Arrows, your Scouters follow a similar three-part training programme. The first part is an 'Initial Training', and then follows the 'Basic Training'. When a Scouter has completed the latter course, he is presented with a green and gold badge or tie pin depicting the Gilwell Emblem (ask Akela to tell you about Gilwell) and a special woggle. Do your Leaders wear these?

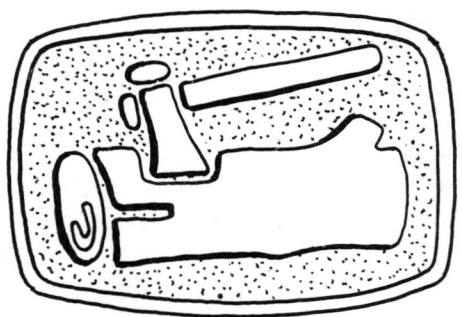

Next there is the 'Advanced Training', which no doubt your Scouter will tell you all about when he is ready to do this, as the Pack have a big part to play in helping the Scouter receive this award.

A Scouter is given several assignments, just as you have assignments for each Arrow, but this time, although the Scouter does the actual planning with perhaps the Sixer's Council, the Pack all have their part to play. This is a very busy time for a Pack because there are so many exciting things to do in just a few months.

How proud you will all feel when your Akela, or Assistant Scouters, receive the Gilwell Scarf and Wood Beads. (In 1889 Baden-Powell fought and captured a Zulu Chief who was wearing a long necklace which consisted of hundreds of beads. These beads were later used for a Scouter's *Wood Badge*. Today the beads are replicas, but there are still some of the original beads in existence.)

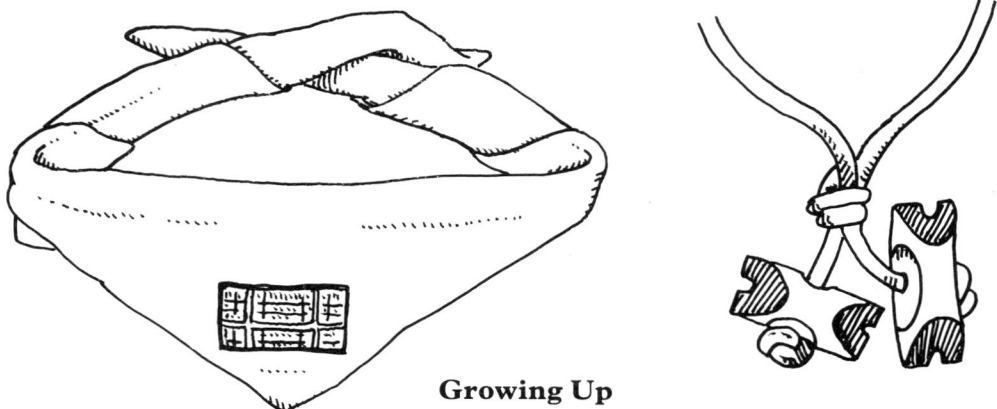

Growing Up

Use a compass and find your way to a secret destination

Early explorers had no compass to help them find their way, but had to rely on the sun, moon and stars.

Supposing you had no compass, how would you find your way in unknown countryside? On a clear night you would have the Pole Star to guide you.

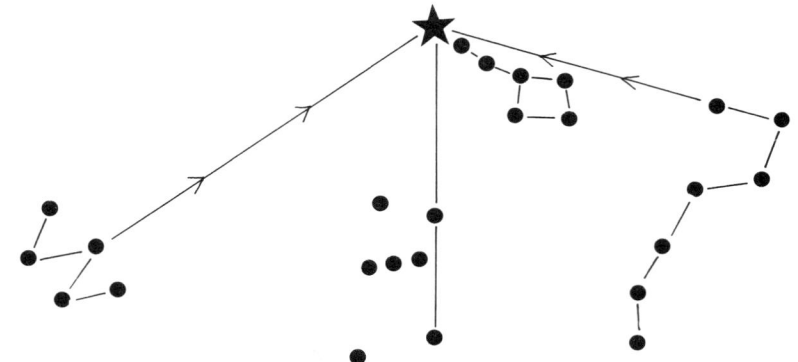

The church is a wonderful compass. There is always one in every village and several in a town. First there is the weather vane. See how many different types you can spot.

In the older type of church, the altar is in the eastern end. Do you know why this is so? It is because the Holy Land where Jesus Christ was born and died, lies in the east.

In old churchyards, the gravestones stand from east to west.

Moss grows on the shady north-northwest side of trees.

Trees lean away from the prevailing wind. What is the prevailing wind in your area?

The sun rises in the east and sets in the west.

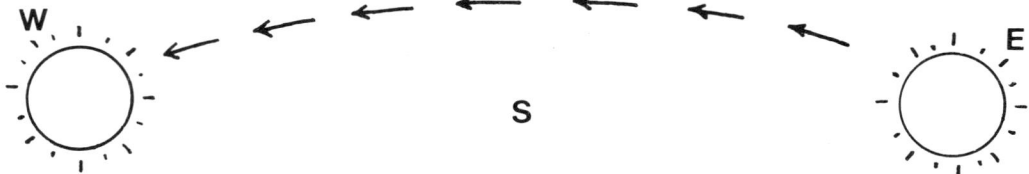

The bark is thicker, and the growth of rings wider-apart on the southern side of a felled tree where there is more warmth and sun.

If your watch is showing the correct time, it makes a very good compass. Hold your watch horizontally and point the hour hand towards the sun. Take no notice of the minute hand. Now imagine a line midway between 12 and the hour hand—this will point due south. (This is Greenwich Mean Time—between October and March. If it is British Summer Time, take an imaginary line between 1 and the hour hand.)

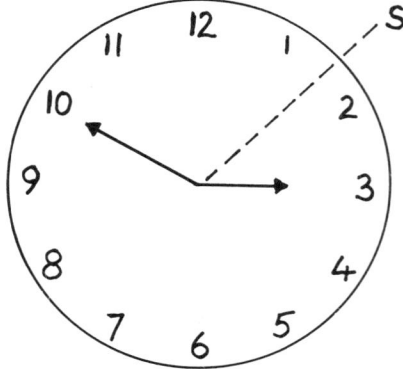

The Compass

The compass is like a watch, but has only one hand which always points north. To use your compass correctly, lay it down on a flat surface and turn the casing until the needle is over the north sign on the dial. Your compass is now 'set'.

Which direction does your house face?

Where does your Scout headquarters lie in relation to your house?

Things to Do

MAKE YOUR OWN WEATHER VANE using either polystyrene tiles or balsa wood.

MAKE A COMPASS

You will need: a darning needle; magnet; small piece of flat cork; small bowl of water.

Hold the needle between finger and thumb and stroke it with one pole of your magnet in the same direction about 30 times.

Float your cork on the water, and carefully lay your needle on it. What happens?

Mark a circular piece of card with eight points of the compass, place it under your bowl and line up the North with your needle.

You now have a homemade compass.

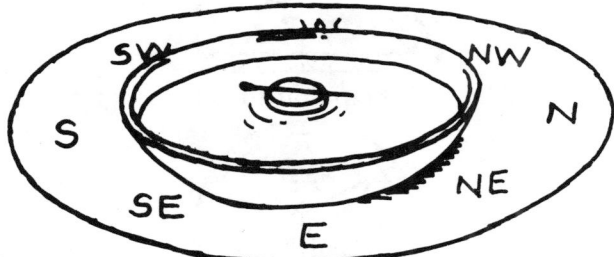

PICTURE COMPASS

Using your house as the centre point, draw eight points of the compass. Then using a map, find a place of interest at each point. See if you can find a small picture of some of these places, or even draw or photograph them.

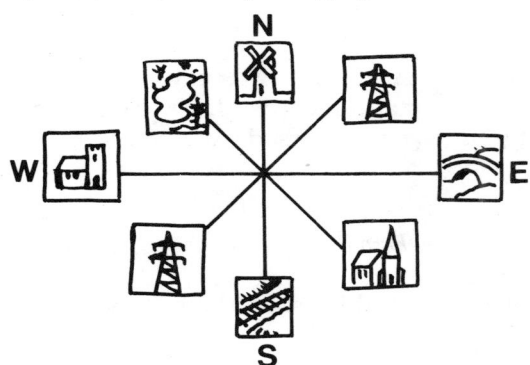

MAKE A WIND CHART

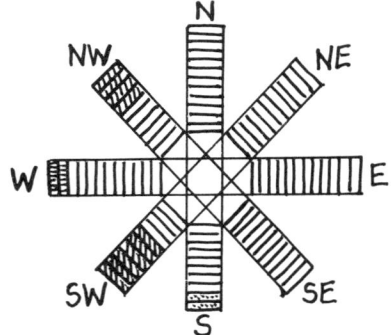

Draw the above on a large sheet of paper, and then colour in one space each day for a month. If the west wind blows, fill in a space on the W arm, and if it is a northwesterly wind, fill in the NW arm and so on.

Suggested colours:

RED   = hot and dry   GREEN   = hot and wet
BLUE = cold and dry   YELLOW = cold and wet

BADGE LINK

The Map Reader Badge will help you to get a great deal of fun out of using your compass.

The Explorer Badge includes finding your way to a place in town or countryside by compass directions.

LINK WITH ANOTHER ARROW ACTIVITY—SHARING

Make your own weather station, with at least two instruments. Keep a log over a period of a fortnight (charts, comments, drawings, etc.).

Growing Up

Make a first aid kit and know how to use the contents. Take it with you on an outing.

The contents of your first aid kit should enable you to give simple first aid to yourself or someone else.

You need a small sturdy box with a secure lid. Something that you can carry in your pocket or rucsac on a Pack or family outing. An empty tin that contained throat tablets is ideal. Mark it clearly on the outside with a red cross, and glue a card with your name, address and doctor's name and telephone number on the inside lid.

Never put anything into your kit that you do not know how to use.

The contents might well depend on the type of expedition you are going on. For example, on a pond dipping evening you would need to include insect repellent. What about these:

Hiking _____

COOKING ON OPEN FIRES _____

A coach journey _____

Exploring the seashore _____

Talk to an adult about what would be most useful to put in your first aid kit.

Always tell your Scouters about any injury you suffer on a Pack outing, even if you have the equipment to deal with it yourself.

CONTENTS

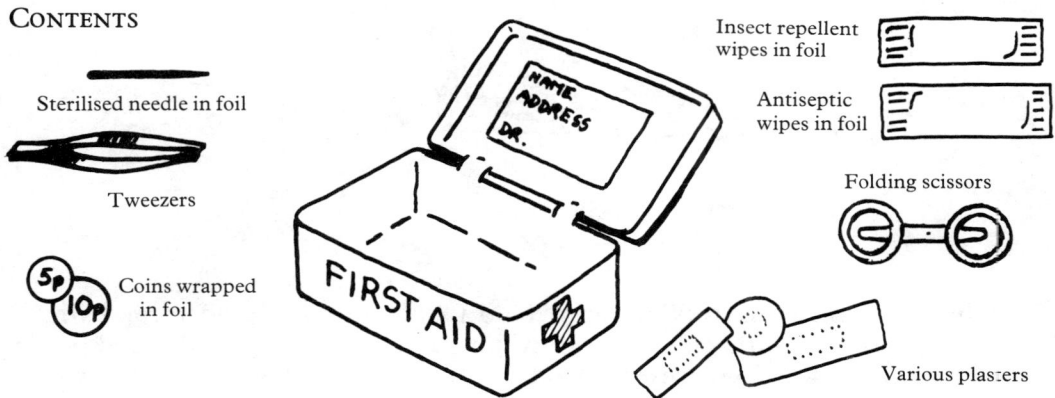

Sterilised needle in foil

Tweezers

Coins wrapped in foil

Insect repellent wipes in foil

Antiseptic wipes in foil

Folding scissors

Various plasters

Antiseptic wipes and Insect Repellent wipes are available from chemists. Many packs contain ten individually sealed wipes.

Your first aid kit is a basic one that will be added to when you become a Scout and then a Venture Scout, for they also carry a first aid kit on all their expeditions.

● Remember to replace any items used from your kit.

Things to Do

● Each Six choose a different location, and then mime an incident that involves using a pretend first aid kit.

B

● Ask Akela to buy 'First Steps in First Aid' for your Pack library. It is published by the St. John Ambulance Association and Brigade. It has 92 pages, and will teach you what to do and what not to do if you come across someone who is hurt.

BADGE LINK

First Aider.

Growing Up

Lay a trail of tracking signs and follow a trail laid by someone else

Following a well laid trail can be great fun, but the laying of tracking signs needs much patience and quite a bit of practice, so start with simple trails.

The rule to remember when laying any trail is that it must not become litter. Make your signs from items that are around you. If it is through woodland, use twigs; on the beach, draw signs in the sand and use pebbles, shells and seaweed as well.

Why not make up a story? Pirates could follow a trail of golden sand which leads them to the treasure; an espionage evening might include a trail of red poster paint mixed with water to represent blood; a woodpecker trail would be of sawdust; a squirrel trail of acorns (but only use when there are no oak trees about). You are sure to think of many more ideas.

A small Pack could follow one trail, but a large Pack would be better having separate trails for each Six. Why not a wool trail of the Six colours? (Beware of green wool in a field or brown in a wood.) These would be for the experienced tracker. The last boy should always pick up the wool.

A blindfold string trail is great fun, and so is a Yeti footprint trail. Why not ask Akela to try one with your Pack?

Now, how far apart should you lay your signs? Perhaps twenty paces is just about right. If you lose the trail, go back to the last sign and mark it with something bright and then spread out and search carefully.

When a wild animal hunts for his prey, he does so by smell. Man's sense of smell is nowhere near as great, so in the past he hunted animals by following their tracks. Pretend you are wild animals and follow a short smell trail. This can be done by rubbing half a peeled onion on to tree trunks.

When you have become an expert with these simple trails, you will then be ready to try the tracking signs below. They are made of materials that suit your locality—stones, twigs, grass, etc. They should be laid in such a way that any member of the public would walk past and not notice them. Remember to keep the signs to one side and not where many feet will kick them aside.

Now go outside and lay a trail for another Six to follow:

This way

Not this way

Gone home

Message hidden 4 paces in direction of arrow

Turn right

Keep going

Things to Do

IN THE COUNTRY

● Whilst out tracking, watch out for animal or bird footprints. The Carousel book 'Tracks, Trails and Signs' by Fred J. Speakman will help you to recognise the various prints.

● See if you can find owl pellets. Owls cannot digest certain parts of their prey, such as bones and feathers, so they cast them up. Look for these at the base of old trees where you think owls might be nesting.

If you are lucky enough to find a pellet, soak it in warm water for a while and then you will be able to take it to pieces very carefully. Mount the pieces on a piece of card. You will then have a display of an owl's diet.

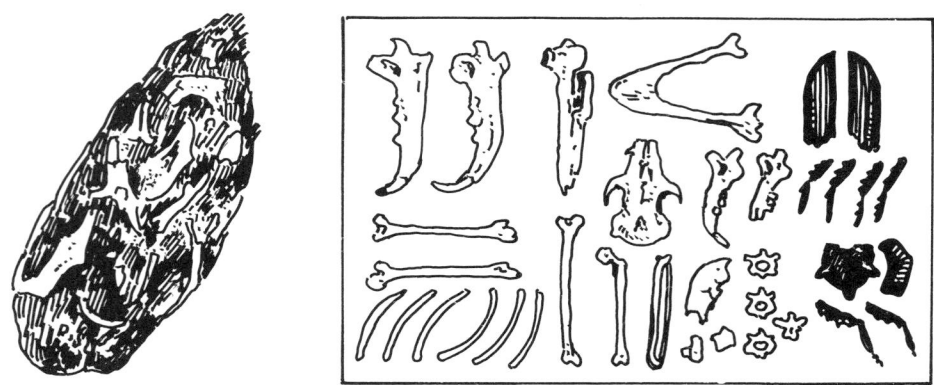

REMEMBER TO WASH YOUR HANDS AFTERWARDS.

IN THE TOWN

● Watch out for manhole covers. Some of these are very old and have a variety of interesting patterns on them. Why not collect rubbings of the various patterns and start a scrap book. All you need is a wax crayon, paper and an old rag to wipe the cover clean.

● To be a good tracker you must learn to be observant. Ask Akela to organise a town or country scavenger hunt.

Growing Up

Go for a walk with an older person and explain how to use the Green Cross Code

1. First find a safe place to cross, then stop.
2. Stand on the pavement near the kerb.
3. Look all round for traffic and listen.
4. If traffic is coming let it pass. Look all round again.
5. When there is no traffic near, walk straight across the road.
6. Keep looking and listening for traffic while you cross.

Do you know which are the safest places when crossing a busy road? Well the best places are pedestrian subways or bridges, but there are not many of these.

The next safest place would be where there is a policeman or 'Lollipop' man on duty.

Then there is the Zebra Crossing. Please do not think that you can walk across in complete safety whenever you like. When you reach a crossing, stand on the pavement near the kerb, and then 'look all round and listen'. Cross only if there is no traffic coming or if the traffic in both directions has stopped to let you cross.

Never cross on the zigzag lines, but always on the black and white stripes.

On some wide busy roads there are refuge places in the middle so that you do not have to cross all the road at once. Remember to use the Green Cross Code before you cross to the refuge and then again before crossing the rest of the road.

Do you have a Pelican Crossing in your town, and do you know how to use it correctly? When you arrive at a crossing, press the button. Watch for the figure of a green man to appear. When it does, remember to make sure that the traffic really has stopped before crossing. If the Green Man starts flashing do not start to cross.

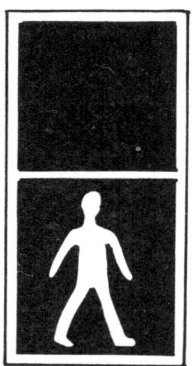
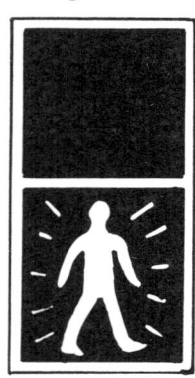

Things to Do

● Fix a large map of your town on the wall of your headquarters. Use blue mapping pins to mark all the places where it is safer to cross the roads. Then use red mapping pins to mark all the dangerous places—the accident black spots.
    Are any of these places on your route to school or Cubs?
● Design a Road Safety Poster, and ask Akela to invite the local Road Safety Officer along to see them, and perhaps he might show you all some films.
● Together with the rest of your Six make recordings of sounds you would hear in the High Street, i.e. car horn, bicycle bell, motorbike, car engine running, etc. Challenge the other Sixes to try and guess what the various sounds are.
● The Highway Code—Read pages 6 to 11, 'The Road User on Foot'.
● Ask at school about the National Cycling Proficiency Training Scheme.

Badge Link

Cyclist Badge

Growing Up

Light a fire out-of-doors and cook something on it

Never light any fire until you have permission from the landowner to do so. If possible, choose a bare piece of ground to make your fire. If this is not possible and you are on a livestock farm, always ask the farmer BEFORE TURFING. Cattle are very curious creatures and will not be satisfied until they have removed the laid turf and made a mess of the area. A livestock farmer might prefer that you burn the grass on a selected area rather than remove the turf.

Use only dead wood—never cut or burn green wood. Girl Guides collect what they call 'punk' to start their fires. Look around for some punk for your fire—dead and dry holly and sweet chestnut leaves, tiny birch twigs and bark, fir cones, pine needles, dry orange peel, shavings, etc.

A small stick pushed into the ground will support your materials.

Around this, make a pyramid of kindling, which are small twigs.

Now gather together wood of various sizes, and grade this in piles near your intended fire. Once your fire is alight, you will want to get on with your cooking and not keep dashing off to find more wood.

Break *dead* wood off trees. It is much drier than wood lying on the ground.

    Your fire should now be ready to light. Shield the fire from the wind, strike the match away from you, and holding it head down, light your fire. After it has caught, the wind will help it to burn. Once it is burning well, add thicker wood until a good fire is going.

● Remember to put the box of matches in a safe dry place away from the fire.

    Don't be tempted to cook your food over roaring flames—you will only end up with a burnt offering for a sausage, and a black and burnt billy if you are cooking popcorn. Wait until the flames have died down. When the embers are glowing red, place your food wrapped in foil into the fire.

    NEVER play with fire and make sure that an adult knows what you are doing—ask Akela or your parents before you start.

HELPFUL TIPS

● If the ground is damp, lay your fire on foil or a platform of sticks.

Wood that burns well for a cooking fire:

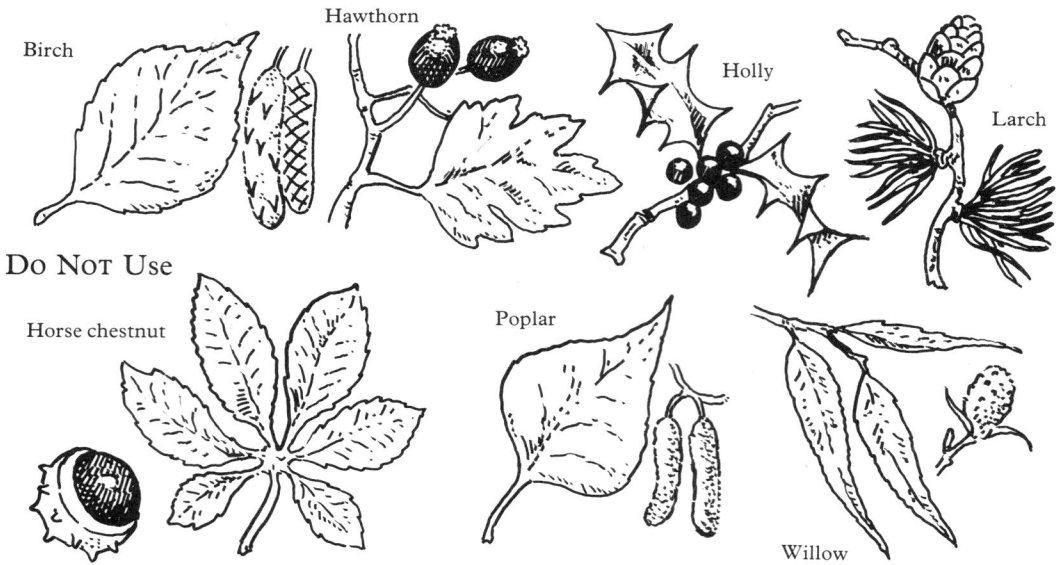

Birch   Hawthorn   Holly   Larch

DO NOT USE

Horse chestnut   Poplar   Willow

T Y P E S   O F   F I R E

Brick fire using a grid from an old cooker.

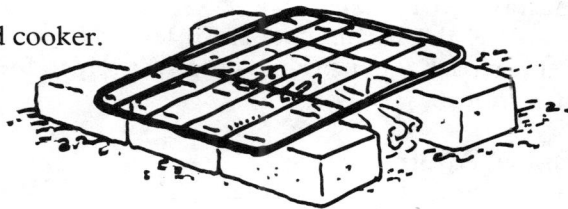

Hunter's fire using two large logs to rest frying pan or billy on.

A fire for sausages and twists on sticks.

C O O K I N G   O N   A   W O O D   F I R E

Popcorn in a Billy

Place a small knob of fat or a little oil in the billy.
When hot, cover base with a single layer of popcorn.
Put a lid on the billy, and listen for popping noises.
Shake the billy slightly until popping stops.
Remove from fire and lift lid. You will find a whole billy full of large puffy popcorn.
Sprinkle sugar over popcorn and share it out with Members of your Six.

Twists

Self raising flour, pinch of salt, small piece of fat rubbed in.
500 g of dough is sufficient for 15 boys.
Mix to a firm dough with water.
Peel the end of a thick green stick, and heat it over the fire. This will dry the sap and help to cook the twist right through.
Roll the flour mixture into a long sausage shape and twist it round the stick in a figure-of-eight.
When it is cooked, it should slide easily off the stick.
Spoon jam into the opening.

Banana Surprise

Peel the banana and slit it lengthways. Insert pieces of chocolate and put the banana back into its skin. Wrap securely in foil and bake in the hot embers for about 10 minutes.

Baked Apple

Core and slit an apple. Fill with brown sugar and sultanas. Wrap in foil and cook in hot embers for about 20 minutes.

Toasted Marshmallows

Cook one or two at a time on sticks over fire.

Sausages

Either on a stick, in foil or in a frying pan.

Don't forget the soup to wash it all down!

CLEARING UP

When the fire has died down, spread the ashes, and either replace soil or sprinkle water on top.

If the ground has been turfed—

add water slowly.

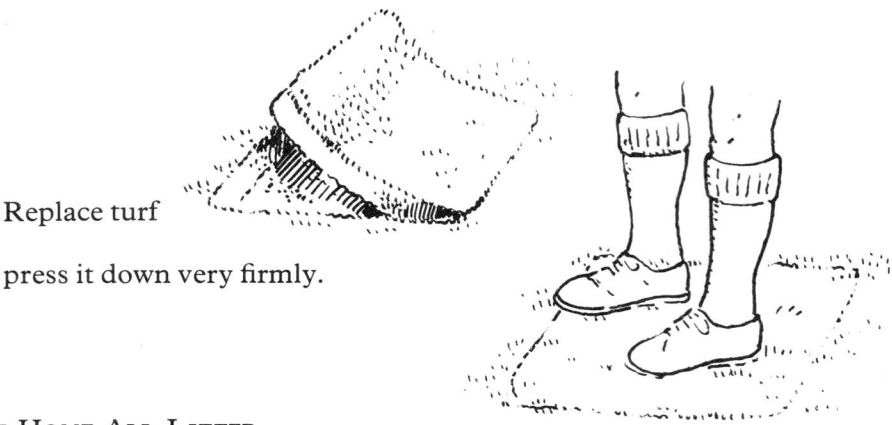

When cold, spread the ashes and stamp down the soil.

Replace turf

press it down very firmly.

TAKE HOME ALL LITTER

Things to Do

- Why not challenge all the Mums to a 'Cook-out' competition evening.
- Make your own cooking pans from foil dishes and wire.
- Try making a toaster from green sticks like this:

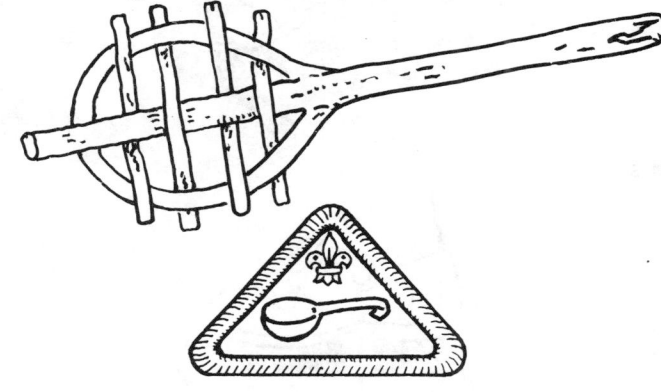

BADGE LINK

Cook

Growing Up
Ride a bicycle safely

Do you own a bicycle or perhaps share one with your brother or sister? Whichever is the case, it is very important that the bicycle you use should be well maintained and is the right height for you.

When you sit on the saddle, you should be able to just touch the ground with both feet, and the 'nose' of your saddle should be tilted very slightly.

The height of the handlebars should be approximately that of your saddle, so that you have to lean slightly forward with your weight shared equally between the handlebars and the saddle.

Always use the ball of your foot:

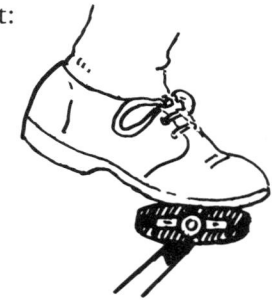

Never like this:

If you use your bicycle to travel to school or to Pack Meetings, do you have a carrier or cycle bag?

Never carry anything that may upset your balance.

BE SEEN—Always wear something bright.

CHECK LIST
- Are all the moving parts oiled?
  Never let any oil get near the brake blocks or wheel frame.
- Is your chain tight enough?
  There should be a maximum play of 2 cm.

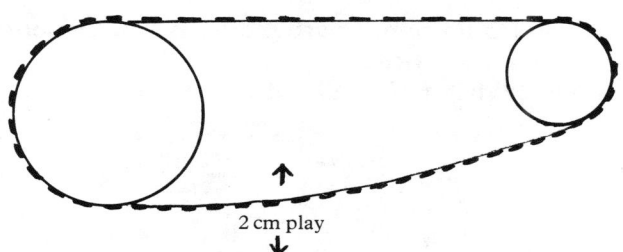

2 cm play

● Have you checked your brake blocks to make sure they are not worn?

When you apply your brakes, the levers should not touch the handlebars. If they do, the brakes will either need adjusting or replacing. When braking, the left or back brake should be applied fractionally before the right or front brake.

● Should you need to stop suddenly because of some emergency.

If you apply your front brake only, this will happen to you:

If you apply just the back brake, this will happen:

● Are your tyres 'happy and hard' or are they 'sad and soft'?

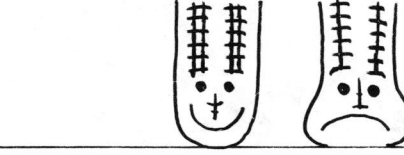

Is the tread in good condition, or are the tyres worn smooth? Tyres must be able to grip the road well in wet weather.

● Are there any bulges or slits in the walls of your tyres?

● Are any spokes missing or loose?
Your wheel will begin to buckle if this happens:

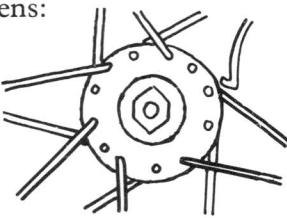

● Is your bell working correctly, and is it placed on the left hand side of your handlebars?
You should be able to ring the bell without taking your hand from the handlebars.

● Is your reflector in place and clean?
ALL BICYCLES MUST HAVE A REFLECTOR BY LAW.

Things to Do

● Hold a 'Cycle Rodeo' evening, i.e., an obstacle race—no free wheeling and remembering to use the balls of your feet; riding between two straight lines; a slow race—last to arrive wins; various relays.

● Give a cycle display for a summer parents' evening. Perhaps formation cycling to music, but this will need a good deal of practice.

● Maybe Akela will ask the Road Safety Officer to come along to a Pack meeting and show you films on cycling, and also to tell you about the National Cycling Proficiency Scheme.

BADGE LINK

Cyclist   Communicator

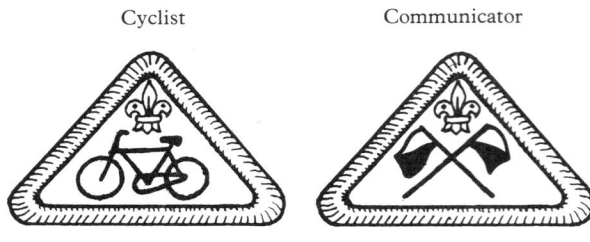

Growing Up

Learn to swim. Discuss the water safety rules with other Cub Scouts or a Leader.

An average of twenty people are drowned every week in Great Britain. Of these seven are children, mostly boys.

In 'Scouting for Boys' Lord Baden-Powell said 'No Scout can be of real use till he can swim, and to learn swimming is no more difficult than to learn bicycling.'

It is very important to be able to swim, but remember, you may be in even more danger than a Cub Scout who cannot swim if you do not know the WATER SAFETY RULES and your own limits.

The following are safety rules that must be followed when swimming in a pool, a river or the sea:

- Always tell your parents where you are going, and NEVER swim alone.
- Keep within your depth.
- Swim in line with the shore and not straight out from the beach.
- Never swim on an empty stomach or within one hour after a heavy meal.
- Never take an airbed into the sea or on lakes. It may take you into deep and unsafe waters.
- Come out of the water before you are too tired or cold, as you may get cramp.
- Always check the area carefully before going for a swim. Do not dive into strange water.
- Never try to duck anybody.

Do you understand the National Colour Code for bathers?

Red Flag

Dangerous for bathing.
Do not enter the water.

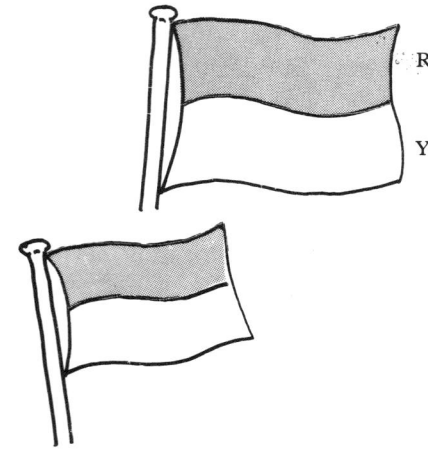

Red

Area patrolled by Lifeguards.

Yellow

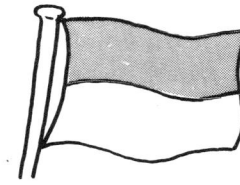

Safe to bathe between flags as area is patrolled by Lifeguards.

White lettering on red board

Conditions dangerous at all times. (Never obscure these signs by hanging your clothes on them.)

Learn to swim correctly, and practise treading water:

Take 'steps' with your feet.

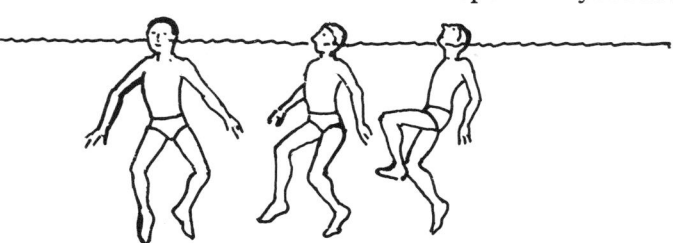

SWIMMING
Front crawl:

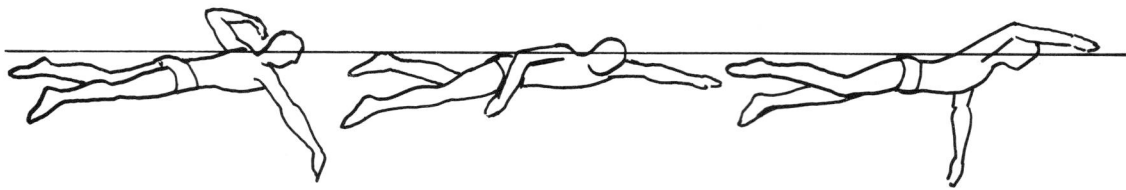

Breast stroke:

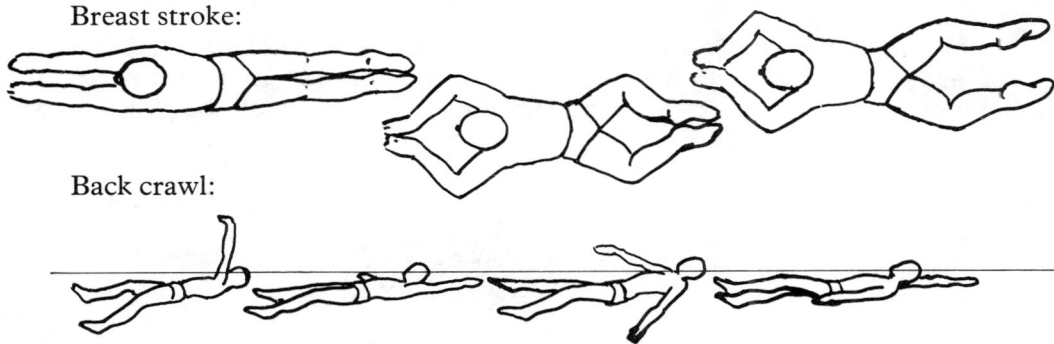

Back crawl:

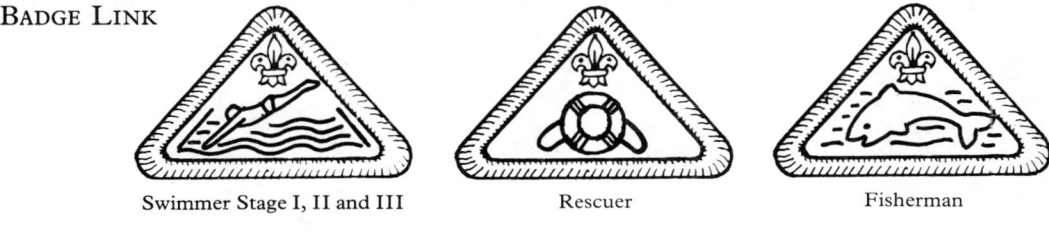

Things to Do

- Visit a Lifeboat Station.
- These are dangerous: gravelpits, canal waters, homemade rafts, playing or ice. Make a poster illustrating one of these dangers.
- With your Six, mime a situation involving one of the Water Safety Rules. Can the rest of the Pack guess which rule it is?

BADGE LINK

Swimmer Stage I, II and III   Rescuer   Fisherman

Growing Up

Know how to apply simple first aid and how and when to get adult help

A Cub Scout who knows how to do basic first aid will be very useful, and the Cub Scout who knows the importance and how to summon adult help may well save a life.

SIMPLE FIRST AID

If possible, always wash your hands before giving first aid.

C

NOSE BLEED

Sit the patient down near some fresh air, and ask him to hold his head forward. Tell him to breathe through his mouth, and then gently pinch the soft part of the nose for a good five minutes. When the bleeding his stopped, tell the patient not to blow his nose for some while.

GRAZES

A graze is bound to be dirty, and may also have some grit mixed in with the dirt. Clean the graze with warm soapy water.

Do not rub, but wipe from the centre of the graze outwards. This will make sure that all dirt and grit are out of the wound.

Cover with adhesive dressing.

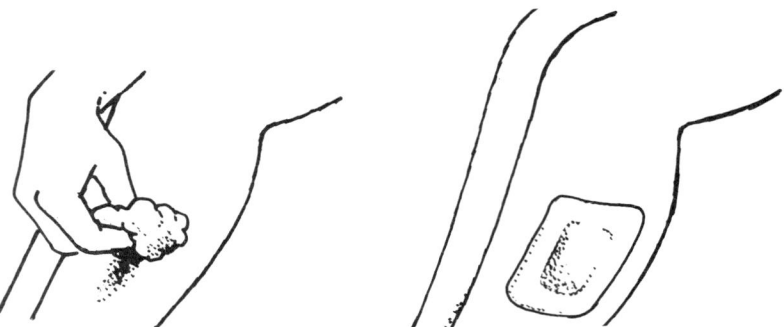

CLOTHING ON FIRE

When a person's clothing catches fire, do not let him rush about or go outside. This will fan the flames. Either douse the flames with water or if no fluid is available hold a rug, blanket, coat or curtain in front of yourself for protection and wrap it closely over the burning area to exclude air. If the fire is starved of oxygen it will quickly go out. Do not use nylon materials to smother the flames, and do not tear off burnt material which is stuck to the skin.

MINOR BURNS AND SCALDS

A BURN is caused by dry heat.

A SCALD is caused by wet heat.

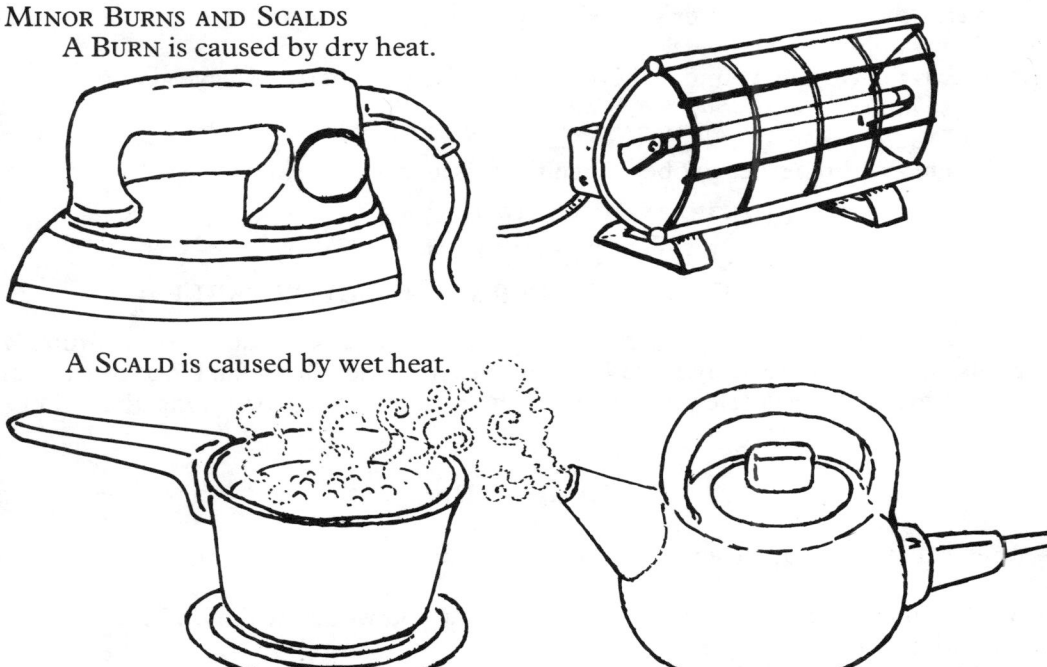

Immediately cool the injured part by pouring cold water over the burn or scald, or holding the limb under a cold tap for *10 minutes*. That is how long it takes to cool the injury.

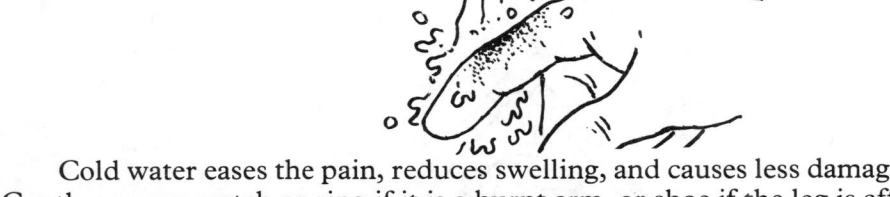

Cold water eases the pain, reduces swelling, and causes less damage to the skin. Gently remove watch or ring if it is a burnt arm, or shoe if the leg is affected. (This is because the injured part of a burn or scald often swells up.)

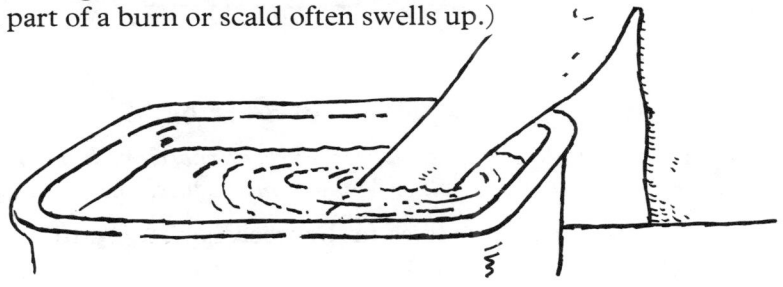

Never prick any blister or germs will get under the skin.
Do not apply any ointment.
Lightly cover the wound if there are any blisters, otherwise leave alone.
If the injury is serious, fetch adult help.

There are three rules to obey when there is an accident:

GIVE FIRST AID TO THE INJURED PERSON
FETCH ADULT HELP QUICKLY
MAKE THE INJURED PERSON COMFORTABLE

In an emergency, it may be necessary to dial 999. You do not need any money for this call. If you are away from home and there is no telephone kiosk near, then trace the wires from a telegraph post to the nearest house, or failing that, shops always have a telephone.

Things to Do

● Invite a doctor, nurse or a St. John Ambulance Officer along to your Pack Meeting.
● With your Six stage an accident and show how you would deal with it.
● Imitation wounds.
    A Graze. Use petroleum jelly and red poster paint. Add some dirt and grit to make it look realistic.
    A Burn. Grease the skin with petroleum jelly and redden with lipstick. Use blobs of petroleum jelly for the blisters.
    Now experiment for yourself on other fake wounds.
● Read 'First Steps in First Aid' published by the St. John Ambulance Association and Brigade.

Badge Link

First Aider

Discovering

Use two of the following in an activity: reef knot, clove hitch, round turn and two half hitches, bowline, highwayman's hitch, hank a short rope

All of us during our lives find ourselves needing to tie a knot apart from the everyday tying of our shoelaces or tying our tie.

But first of all—what *is* a knot? Well, the dictionary says 'a knot is a means of tying two pieces of rope together and making sure that they stay secure and do not slip'.

When practising your knots, always use a good rope and never just odd pieces of string and, remember, the rope should always be long enough for proper use. It is much easier to learn a knot from one of your Scouters and not from a book. Stand by the side of them and not in front, otherwise you will find yourself trying to do everything backwards.

If you learn your knots well in the Cub Scout Pack, when you become a Scout it will be easier to learn the various lashings that the Troop use for bridge building, constructing camp gadgets and making rafts, etc.

In 'Scouting for Boys' Lord Baden-Powell says 'The right kind of knot to tie is one that you can be certain will hold under any amount of strain, and which you can always undo easily if you wish to. A bad knot is one which slips away when a hard pull comes on it, or which gets jammed so tight that you cannot untie it.'

Who are the people that use knots as part of their job, or need to know the right kind of knot otherwise their lives would be in danger if they used a loose incorrect knot that slipped undone?

Well, there are the yachtsmen. Can you find out what knots they use? Perhaps Akela knows a keen yachtsman who would come along to your Pack Meeting.

Have you a Cub who has gained his Fisherman's Badge in the Pack? If so, maybe he will show you the knots he uses.

What about the farmer? Imagine what would happen to that high load of straw or hay bales if it were not tied securely with the correct knot, or if a cow was tied up in the loose box awaiting the vet and managed to pull the knot which held her undone. Rural Packs could visit a farm and learn the correct knots on the spot.

Do you know someone whose hobby is climbing? Perhaps your Group has a Venture Scout Unit whose Members are enthusiastic climbers and who would be willing to come and show you what knots they use.

How many other people can *you* think of who rely on the correct use of knots?

KNOTS
The Reef Knot

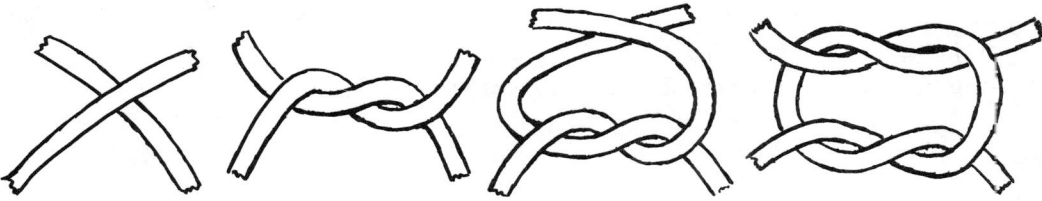

A reef knot is used for bandaging because it lies flat. It is also used for tying up parcels.

Things to Do

1. Each Six act out an incident, i.e. falling off a bicycle and cutting a knee, or taking part in sports and straining an ankle. Put on a temporary bandage using a reef knot.

2. Make a parcel by tying up a book with brown paper and string. Each Six to be Post Office Sorting Staff and have a relay taking it in turns to throw your parcel to your Sixer and back. How many parcels would never reach their destination?

CLOVE HITCH

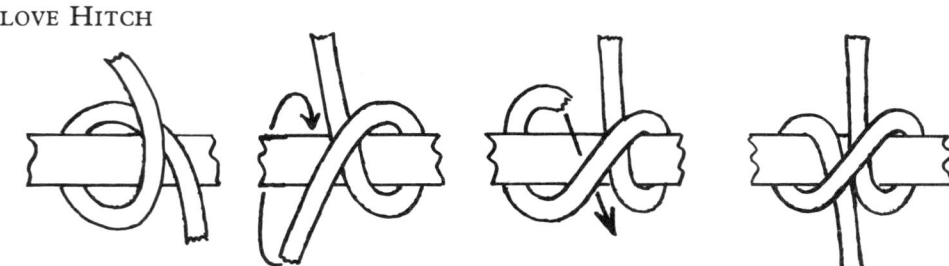

Scouts use a clove hitch at the beginning and end of some lashings. It is also used for fastening a rope to a spar because either end will keep firm without slipping if the strain is the same on either side.

Learn both the simple way of slipping the two loops over the end of the pole, and the other way when the first cannot be used.

ROUND TURN AND TWO HALF HITCHES

This knot is usually used for tying a rope to a pole. It is ideal for making a washing line for Mum, or making a boat fast to the bank.

Things to Do

Make a washing line, and have a relay hanging up the washing. Does your line hold?

BOWLINE

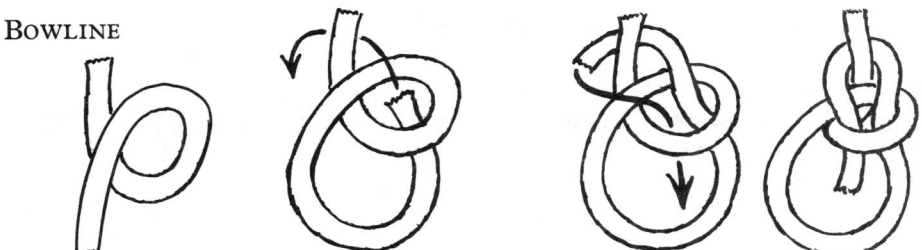

A bowline is a loop which will not slip, and will hold fast under great strain. This seems to be the most difficult knot to learn, but with practice, you will be able to tie it quite quickly. Always tie it round yourself when you are learning. Then try tying it round someone else.

Things to Do

Two exciting Pack Meetings could be: 'Preparing to Climb Everest' and then 'Conquering Everest'.

HIGHWAYMAN'S HITCH

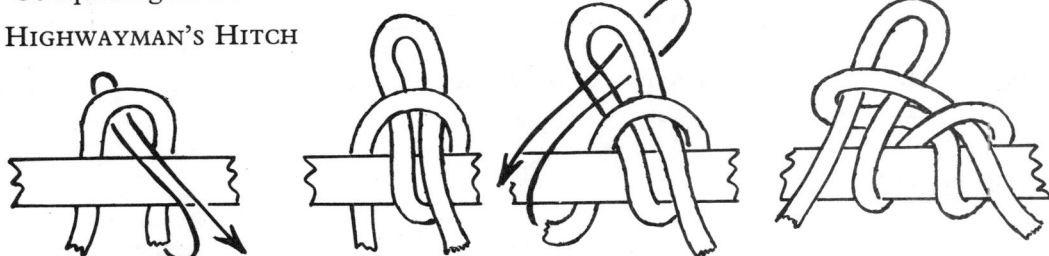

A hitch secures a rope to another object. You will find the Highwayman's Hitch great fun to learn.

Things to Do

If you have a Cowboy and Indian evening, use this hitch to tether your 'horse' and then see which one of you can make the quickest get-away.

HANK A ROPE

Always put your rope away tidily when you have finished with it, and never leave it lying about to become tangled and frayed.

Coil a piece of rope remembering to leave some spare in order to fasten the hank. Fasten like this:

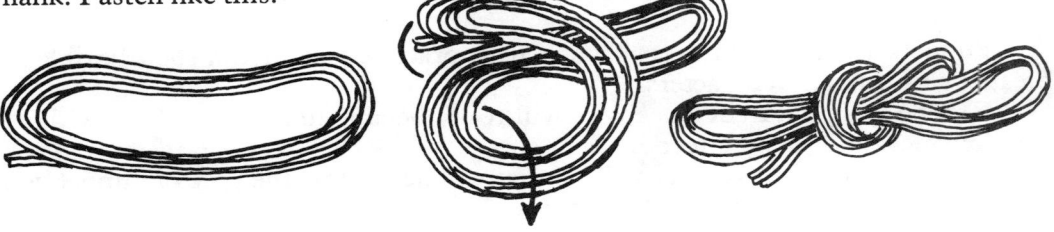

Things to Do

● Read the Ladybird book 'Learn about Knots'.
● Make a 'doing' knotting board. Make the knots with coloured rope if possible and fasten them to your board. Alongside each knot hang pieces of rope fastened to a loop for any Cub to practise the various knots.
● Challenge another Six to a knotting quiz:

1. This knot makes a large arm sling a great deal more comfortable _____

2. A cowboy could make a quick get-away with this knot_____

3. To prepare the Union Flag for breaking, you need to know this knot _____

4. The Scouts use this knot to start and finish some of their lashings_____

5. You can tie a boat up securely with this knot_____

6. This knot is used to prevent your rope from becoming tangled _____

Answers: Reef knot; highwayman's hitch; sheetbend; clove hitch; round turn and two half hitches; short hank.

● Macramé: With just the reef and clove hitch, you can make a belt for yourself with coloured string. There are a number of books showing various patterns.
● Why not work out some magic string tricks to entertain the Pack?
● Ask Akela to show you how to make 'Cats' Cradles'. This involves making a string pattern and then passing it from one person to another making a different pattern each time. Altogether there are eight patterns.
● If you go on holiday to a fishing resort, keep your eyes open for fishermen mending their nets. Try making a small net yourself.

Discovering

Make a puppet and take part in a puppet play

Puppets are great fun to make, and with practice you should soon be able to create many different characters.

Hidden from your audience, you will really be able to let yourself go with all sorts of voices and sound effects.

But first, what will you need? Well that will depend on the type of puppet you have in mind, so let us see what there are.

There are the dish mop and wooden spoon puppets:

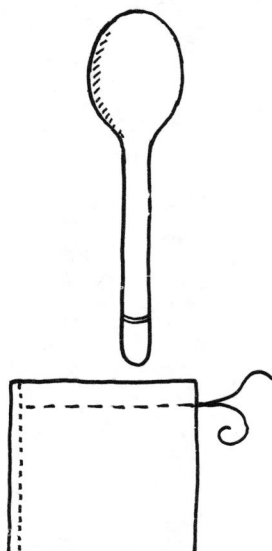

Wool

Felt tips for features

Pipe cleaners or rolled paper for arms

A strip of material with short sides glued or sewn with a needle and long thread. Make long stitches round top edge. Fit on puppet and pull thread tight and knot. Wrap matching material round arms and top of body.

Dish Mop Witch

Dish mop for head

An empty plastic lemon for face

Black material for cloak

Black paper for hat

An apple makes an excellent face because as it ages, it makes a perfect witch's face, all wrinkled and ugly. Use plasticine for the ears and hooked nose.

Paper plate puppets are very easy to make:

Eyebrows of pieces of fur

Button eyes

Painted mouth

A stick fixed at the back with tape

Match Box Puppets

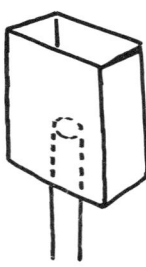

Two circles of card about 8 cm in diameter.
One representing a happy face and the other a sad one.
Arms can be rolled paper.

Sock Puppets. Socks can be made into all sorts of animals:

A piece of cardboard same length as foot of sock

    Place the card into the sock, and push your hand into the foot with the thumb pressing into the heel and the rest of the fingers into the toe.

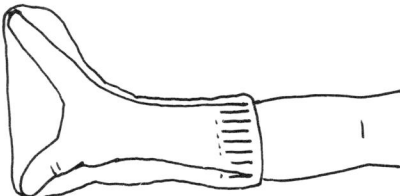

Close your hand, and ask someone to sew each corner of the mouth.

Add features and maybe a tongue.

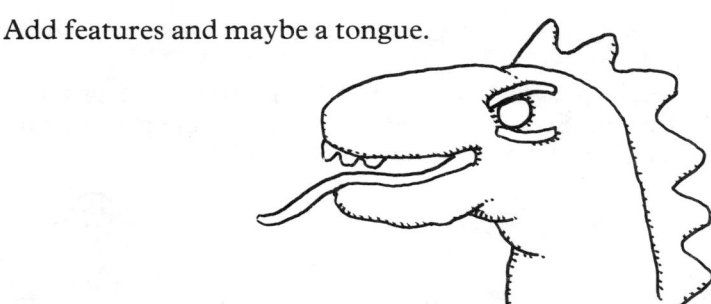

Glove Puppet. Heads can be modelled from papier-mâché, but this is more involved and takes time to dry.

Why not use an old ball, and cover it with a white sock.

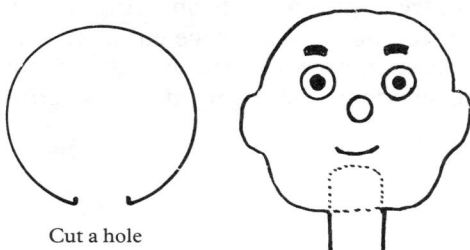

Put padding inside the sock for the ears and nose and stitch in place before fastening the neck.

Cut a hole

Roll a tube of thin card about the size of your first finger, and fix it inside the head.

Puppet Glove Template. Fold a piece of card in half and place your hand with the second finger on the fold and your thumb extended. Carefully draw round your hand and down nearly to your elbow, allowing at least 2 cm all round for when you sew up the glove. Cut it out, unfold and place on a double piece of material.

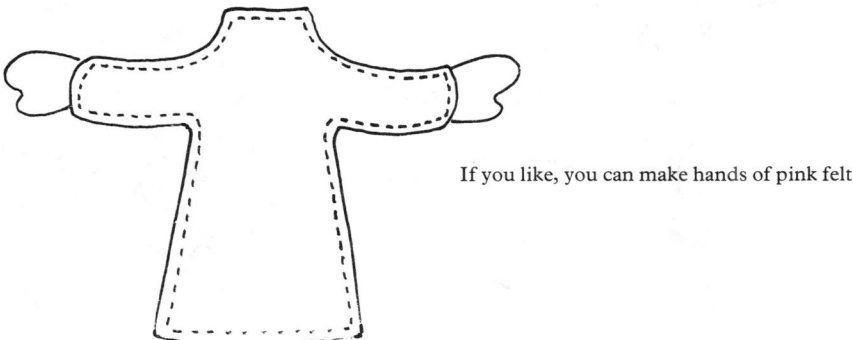

If you like, you can make hands of pink felt

Yoghurt Carton Puppets. A ping-pong ball on a garden cane; one yoghurt carton; a piece of material about 25 cm × 20 cm.

Fold the material, and sew down the longest side. Turn right side out, gather the top and tie round the neck of the puppet. Make a hole in the bottom of the yoghurt carton, and push the cane through. Gather bottom of material under the yoghurt carton and glue in place.

If the whole Six work together, perhaps you could produce '10 Little Cub Scouts' and write a special verse for them on Highway Code, Country Code or Water Safety.

Shadow Puppets. Make very simple shapes on cardboard. Cut out, and attach a garden cane with tape. You will need to make a screen of old white sheeting. Lay a large tablecloth over a table. Turn two chairs upside down, and place either end of the table. Fix the sheet between the chairs. Darken the room, and switch a table lamp on behind the screen. Hold the puppets up against the sheeting and make sure *your* shadow is not cast on it!

Tell the story of Jonah and the Whale with shadow puppets:

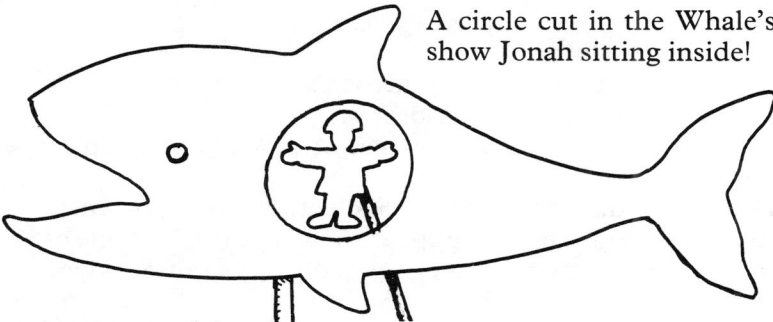

A circle cut in the Whale's stomach will show Jonah sitting inside!

Monsters can be made with padded coat hangers and trimmings of cardboard. The head will move most realistically.

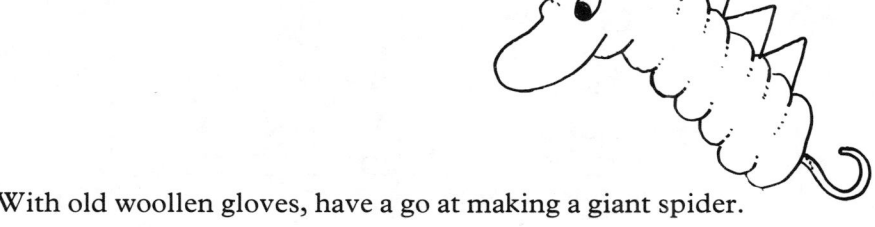

With old woollen gloves, have a go at making a giant spider.

Whatever puppets you decide to make, do not forget the sound effects and perhaps the appropriate music.

An ideal puppet theatre would be a large cardboard box:

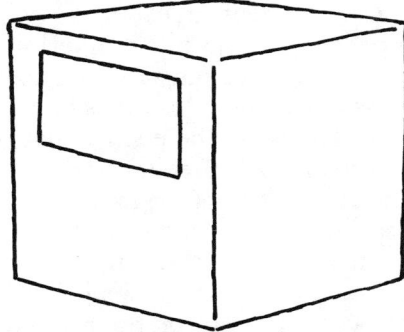

but two chairs standing on a table with a curtain to hide behind will do.

Things to Do

● Make puppets to fit in with other Arrow activities, i.e. International, home safety, people who have done their best, 100-word story, etc.
● If you are working on the Handyman Badge, perhaps you can make a more permanent theatre.
● Make up a play, and with the rest of your Six, entertain your parents.
● Perhaps each Six could give a short puppet show on the life of one of our Saints. Just think what a wonderful dragon you could create to fight St. George in all his shining armour!
● Read 'The Know How Book of Puppets' published by Usborne Publishing Ltd. It is full of colourful illustrations and good ideas.

BADGE LINK

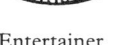

Entertainer

Handyman

Discovering

Think up and use a secret code

Sending a secret message to your friends can be very exciting, and if adults are unable to read it, this can make it doubly exciting.

Codes are used throughout the world by the Army, Navy and Air Force in peacetime as well as in war, and ambassadors of all countries send all their confidential reports to their Governments in code.

A war can be won, not because of one side's superior weapons, but on whether vital messages in code manage to get through safely to the officer in charge.

In 'Scouting for Boys', Baden-Powell describes how a Captain, unable to reach his troops to warn them of an attack by the enemy that night, saw an old railway engine nearby and lit a good fire in her. When it had got up steam, the Captain blew the whistle with the short and long blasts of the morse code. The army were alerted, and the 20,000 troops were saved from a surprise attack.

Morse was never meant to be used for written messages, but was invented to be sent by telegraph. You can send messages to a friend by long and short flashes with a torch or even whistle or tap your message on the ground with a stick. If you want to pass a secret message to a friend close at hand, try winking the morse code—one eye for a dot, and two eyes for a dash. Instead of writing the morse code in dots and dashes, try a much quicker way using short and long strokes:

Akela is coming

Of course, millions of people all over the world know about the morse code, so it does not make a very secret message does it?

An easy code would be to divide your words up in a completely different way:

RE DSI XMU STREP OR TTOA KELA
RED SIX MUST REPORT TO AKELA

or even write your words backwards like this:

DER XIS TSUM TROPER OT ALEKA

or add a dummy first letter like this:

ARE BDSIXMU CSTREP DOR ETTOA FKELA

You can invent a code of your own something like this:

A ☐

B ▫

C ☐☐

D ▫▫   and so on.

Or by using a typewriter, come up with something like this:

A   %

B   ★

C   @

D   =   and so on.

However these codes have one disadvantage, you either have to remember the symbols or carry a copy with you. They also take time to decode.

Here is an interesting cipher called the Pig-pen cipher. Begin by drawing four patterns:

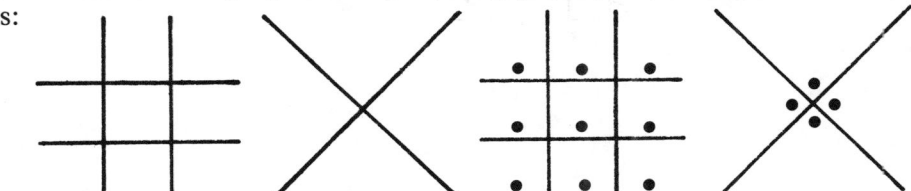

Now write in the letters of the alphabet:

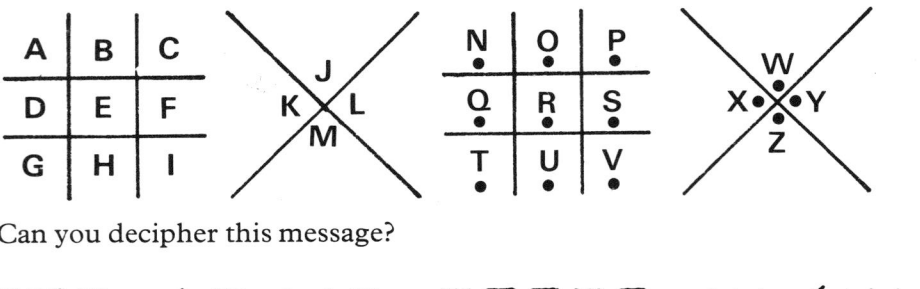

Can you decipher this message?

∧☐☐⅂ ∧☐ I⅃⅂ ⅂∩⊡☐☐ ⅃L<⅃L>

Now try some sentences of your own.

Can you understand this:

ALLWAY UBCAY COUTSSAY ILLWAY ENJOYWAY HISTAY.

This is a spoken code called Pig Latin. It has nothing to do with pigs or Latin, but is a secret language which can be mastered very quickly. You just add WAY to all words beginning with A E I O U. For all other words you just move the first letter to the end and add AY.

Find out if someone in your Six also wants to learn Pig Latin, and then start talking together. Use short simple sentences to start with, and then gradually speed up.

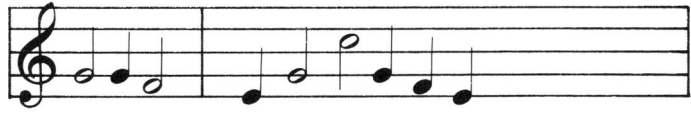

If you wrote a message this way, anyone who couldn't read music would just think it was a nice jingle.

Key to the musical cipher:

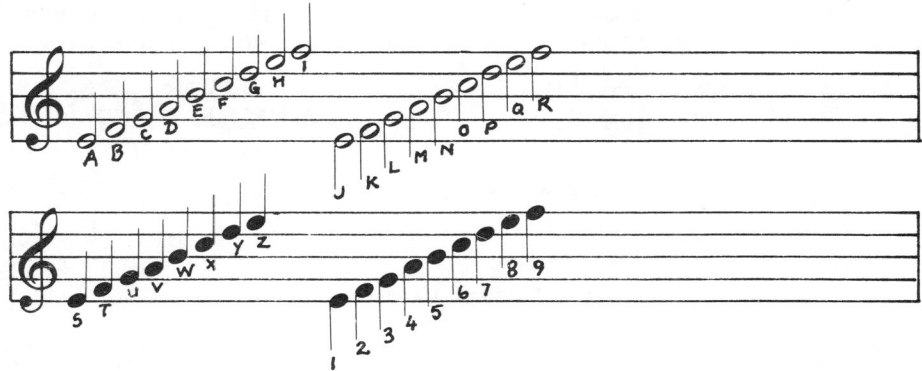

Numbers can be used instead of letters:

A B C D E F G etc. or number backwards A B C D E F G etc.
1 2 3 4 5 6 7   26 25 24 23 22 21 20

If you and your friend both have a similar book, these can become your special code books. For example, supposing you both have the Ladybird book 'Learnabout Knots'—you might send this message:

4/5/4   6/1/3   7/4/1   8/4/5   9/2/12   11/1/11   16/1/4

The first number gives the page, the second, the line and the third gives the word.

It is not easy to break a code, and a great deal of patience is needed. To help you to decipher a message:

the most common letters in the English Alphabet are

E   T   A   O   N

and the most common words are

THE   AND   TO   IN   AT.

If you have a coded message to deliver to someone, where will you hide it?

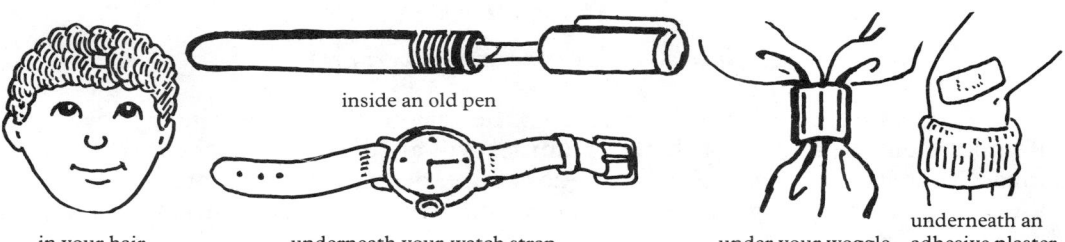

in your hair   underneath your watch strap   under your woggle   underneath an adhesive plaster

D

How many places can you think up?

You might decide to make your message even more secret by writing it in invisible ink. The message must be written carefully, and certainly never with a scratchy pen. Use an old cartridge pen or a used match sharpened at one end with sandpaper. Try some of the following, and then think up some of your own:

MILK (not the cream)   VINEGAR
SUGAR OR HONEY   LEMON JUICE
POTATO JUICE   ONION JUICE

All these are developed with heat. An electric light bulb or an iron are best. NEVER WORK WITH AN OPEN FLAME OR FIRE.

Things to Do

● Read 'The Know How Book of Spycraft' by Falcon Travis and Judy Hindley (Usborne Publishing Ltd.); 'The Good Spy Guide' by the same authors and publisher; 'Codes and Secret Writing' by Herbert S. Zim (Piccolo).
● Ask Akela if he will organise some spy or espionage evenings for the Pack.
● Make your own identikit file. Collect large pictures of faces from colour magazines and cut across the faces separating the hair, eyebrows, eyes, etc.
● Gather together a collection of different types of footwear: Wellington boots, flip flops, football boots, plimsols, flippers, etc. Make prints with poster paint, then try to match the shoe to the print.
● Match the finger prints. Each Member of your Six makes two prints of the right thumb. Jumble all the prints and then try to pair them up.

BADGE LINK

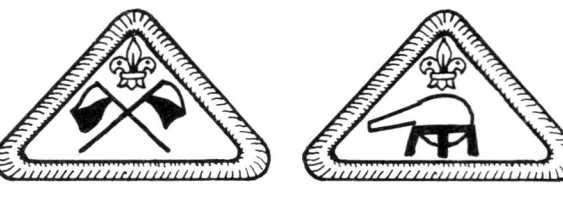

Communicator   Scientist

Discovering

Carry out three scientific experiments

Ideas for experiments can come from the various Pack Meetings. For example, if you are having a spy month opportunities will arise to experiment with invisible inks. Programmes on airliners bring ideas for experiments concerning air, wind or flight. If you are giving a puppet show, you may need special lighting effects with bulbs and batteries.

During the summer months, many experiments can be carried out with plants: excluding light; or watching water skaters on a pond and experimenting with water tension.

AIR

Make gliders from various materials: paper, card, polystyrene, balsa wood, etc. What keeps them up? Which flies the furthest? Why?

STREAMLINING

Carry out this experiment:

What happens? Why?

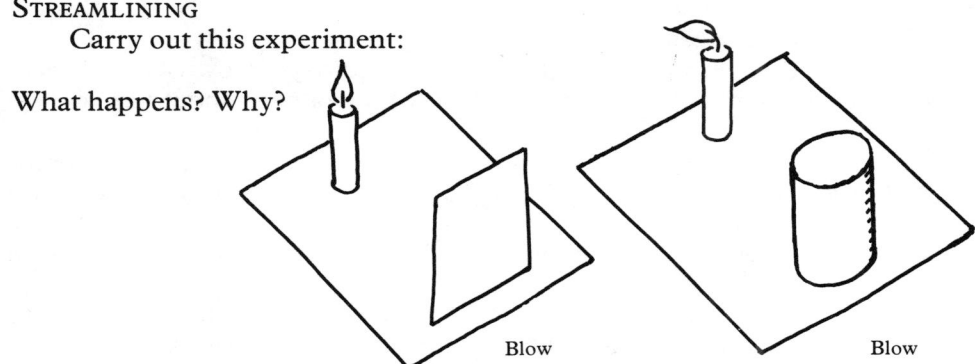

Look at pictures of old and new forms of transport. Design your own streamlined car or airliner.

Have you read about Sir Alexander Fleming's experiments concerning the discovery of penicillin? Why not carry out your own experiment on growing mould. You can use stale bread, cooked potato, beetroot, jam, etc. Look at it each day. What do you think is happening? If possible, study the growth under a microscope or magnifying glass. (The woman who helped Fleming in his work was nicknamed 'Mouldy Mary' because she was always going into shops and asking for mouldy or stale food.)

ALEXANDER GRAHAM BELL

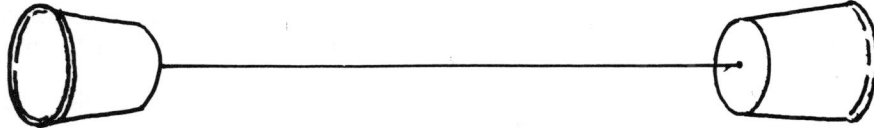

Make a telephone from two cream cartons and a piece of thin string. Your friend speaks into his carton, and you hold your carton to your ear. Does your telephone work better with the string stretched tightly or hanging loosely? How far will the sound travel? Does the thickness of the string make any difference?

Now, what do you know about Albert Einstein, Sir Isaac Newton, Michael Faraday and Samuel Morse. Carry out some experiment connected with each of these.

A YEAST PLANT

If your mother or grandmother makes her own bread, ask if you can have three teaspoonfuls of dried yeast. Place three clean yoghurt cartons on the table, and put one teaspoonful of yeast into each one. Now fill two of the cartons half full with warm water (not hot or it will kill the yeast). Add one teaspoonful of sugar to *one* of these. Wait for 30 minutes. What has happened.

Why do you think the carton with yeast, water and sugar is so frothy and bubbly? (The sugar feeds the yeast plants, and as the plants grow more yeast plants are produced and they give off carbon dioxide gas and alcohol. The bubbles are therefore of carbon dioxide gas.)

Why not look up a recipe for Ginger Beer and start your own Ginger Beer plant. It is as exciting to make as it is to drink, and you will need about $\frac{1}{2}$ oz yeast to 5 pints of water.

Did you know that you breathe out carbon dioxide? Did you, therefore, know that if your class at school or your Cub Scout Pack sat in a closed room they would soon begin to feel very sleepy and perhaps develop a headache? That is why we must always have a window open to bring in the fresh air that we all need—a mixture of oxygen and nitrogen.

Try this experiment: Heat the wax at the end of a candle, and fix it safely on to a saucer. Fill the saucer with water and then light the candle. Place a jam jar over the candle and watch what happens. Use a larger jar. Is there any difference?

Suppose the Pack was learning about how men first told the time or exploring space (Discovering), think how interesting it would be to try out some experiments.

A CANDLE CLOCK

You will need a block of wood with two nails driven into it about 5 cm apart. Lay the wood down with nail points uppermost.

Push a candle securely on to each nail.

Light one candle, and when five minutes have elapsed, mark the other candle at the same level. Continue this every five minutes until the candle has burned out. Mark circles round the unlit candle with a felt pen, and you now have a *Candle Clock*.

Work out for yourself how you can make:

a sand glass (something on the lines of an old-fashioned egg timer)

a water clock (these were used by the Greeks and Romans)

a sundial

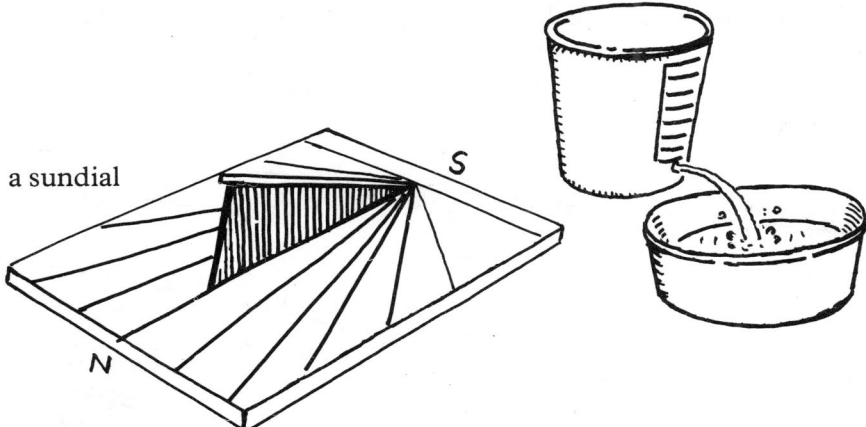

a chiming clock (you don't have to see a clock to tell the time)

Things to Do

● Read the Ladybird books: 'Magnets and Electricity'; 'Light'; 'Air'.
● Read Leonard De Vries three books of experiments (Corgi; Carousel) and astound your friends with your own magic show.

BADGE LINK

Scientist   Entertainer

Discovering

Make a plaster cast of an animal's or bird's footprint. Discuss its way of life with other Cub Scouts or a Leader.

MATERIALS YOU WILL NEED
    Strips of card to make a collar to place round the print.

Paper clips hold the collar in place.

Two margarine tubs. One with a lid to keep the Plaster of Paris moisture proof.

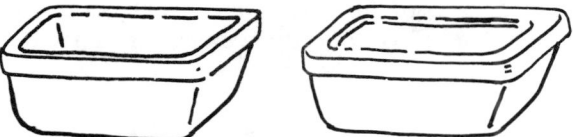

Plaster of Paris—Dental Plaster of Paris is best. It is a very fine and white powder which sets quickly and strongly. It can be obtained from almost any chemist.

Bottle of water.

Newspaper.

WHAT YOU DO

First find your print. You will be unlikely to find any prints after a long period of dry weather. The perfect print is not easy to find. If you discover several prints of an animal or bird, walk beside them so as not to disturb them, and choose the one that is not spoilt by a stone or leaves. Now place a wall of cardboard round your print and fix it into shape with the paper clip. Press the circle into the earth being careful not to disturb the print.

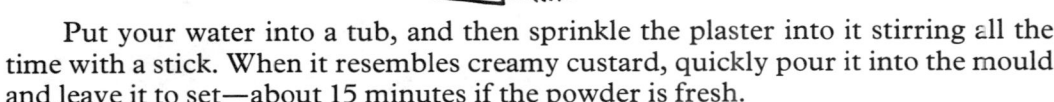

Put your water into a tub, and then sprinkle the plaster into it stirring all the time with a stick. When it resembles creamy custard, quickly pour it into the mould and leave it to set—about 15 minutes if the powder is fresh.

Gently feel the plaster periodically to see if your cast is set. Your cast will first become very warm, and then cool. Only then is it safe to take up from the soil. Wrap it in newspaper to take home. This not only keeps your cast safe, but helps to dry up any excess moisture.

Next day, place the cast under running water and gently rub the mud off the mould with an old toothbrush. When it is dry, you can paint it.

You now have a negative impression. Should you want a positive cast, first brush the negative with soapy water, place a collar round it, and pour in some freshly mixed plaster. Leave it to set for 15 minutes and then pull apart.

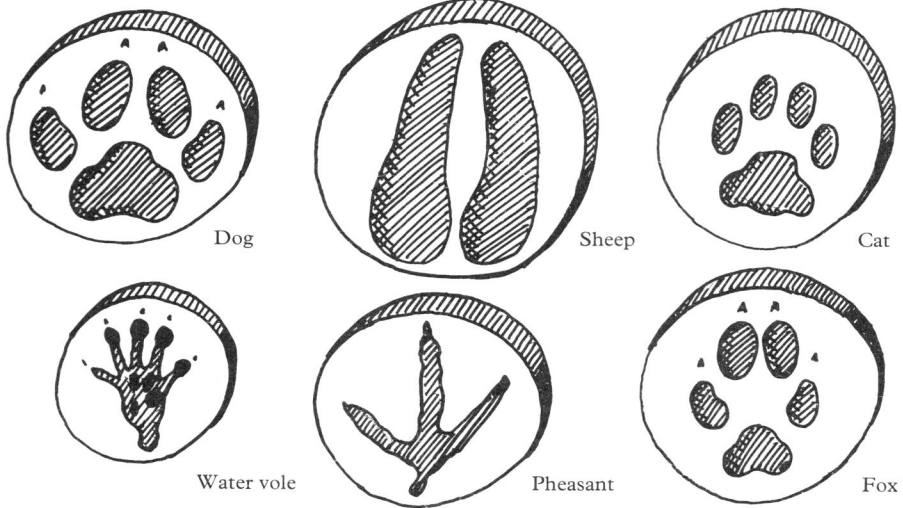

Dog   Sheep   Cat

Water vole   Pheasant   Fox

The best place to find bird tracks, are along a stream or river or by the side of a lake.

The Heron has his favourite spot where he will stand silently on one leg watching for unsuspecting fish to swim by.

The Coot prefers lakes to the slow moving streams or ponds.

Watch out for the Great Crested Grebe, which is one of our most colourful birds.

To make a cast along a muddy river bank, mix the plaster of Paris and water to a thinner consistency so as not to destroy the print.

Remember to label your plaster cast with the name, date and where it was found.

There are many books giving information on animals and birds. Among them are three Ladybird books: 'British Wild Animals'; 'Pond and River Birds'; 'Birds and How They Live'.

To learn more about tracks and trails, read the Carousel book: 'Tracks, Trails and Signs' by Fred J. Speakman, ISBN 0552 540765.

Things to Do

● You can have fun making shoe or Wellington boot prints of yourself and friends; or maybe a print from your dad's car tyre.

● Why not make casts of tree barks. Use either softened clay or plasticine about 8 cm by 10 cm and 2 cm thick. Place it on to your chosen trunk, and press it hard to obtain a good impression.

Remove the clay or plasticine very carefully, and place a cardboard collar round it. Pour the Plaster of Paris mixture into the mould and leave to set. Finally paint your cast and label.

● Make leaf prints. Vaseline the underside of your leaf. Spread a 1 cm thickness of mixed plaster of Paris over a postcard. After a minute, lay the leaf on to the plaster. When set, lift the leaf and you have your print. Paint and label it.

● Ask Akela to send for the plastic Scout Badge moulds from SCOUTING Magazine. You can then make your own wall plaques or Six Trophy.

BADGE LINK

World Conservation Badge

Discovering

Find out about the three crosses of the Union Flag and learn the National Anthem. Know what to do when flags are flown and National Anthems played.

Many countries have a National Anthem. The National Anthem of Great Britain is called 'God Save the Queen'.

The Queen is the head of our country, so when we hear the National Anthem played we should stand smartly at the alert and try to think of what the words mean to us.

You will notice that in the last verse we sing 'may she defend our laws', meaning the laws of our country, just as you promise to keep the Law of the Cub Scout Pack. So you see that everyone of us, from the Queen down to the smallest Cub has a duty to do for our country.

How many occasions can you think of when the National Anthem is played?

> God save our gracious Queen,
> Long live our noble Queen,
> God save the Queen.
> Send her victorious,
> Happy and glorious,
> Long to reign over us;
> God save the Queen.
>
> Thy choicest gifts in store
> On her be pleased to pour,
> Long may she reign.
> May she defend our laws,
> And ever give us cause
> To sing with heart and voice
> God save the Queen.

Flags have a very long history. They were taken into battles, especially during the Crusades. They used to mark the position of leaders and form a rallying point for the soldiers.

The Union Flag is the emblem of Great Britain and Northern Ireland. Cub Packs and Scout Troops fly the flag at their meetings and camps, and it is also flown on special days like birthdays of the Royal Family.

The flag should be flown with the broad white line at the top nearest the flagpole. If it is flown the other way round it is a sign of distress.

If a member of the Royal Family or a Head of State dies the flag is flown at half-mast.

The Union Flag is made up of the following flags:

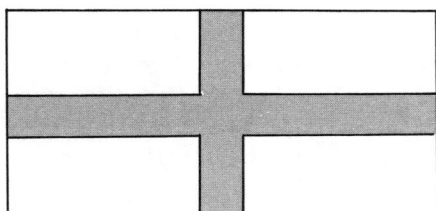

St. George of England

Saint's Day: 23rd April
Emblem of England: Rose

For centuries, the National Flag of England has been the red cross on a white field.

Saint's Day: 30th November
Emblem of Scotland: Thistle

St. Andrew of Scotland

It is believed that the cross on which Andrew was crucified was diagonal.

When James VI of Scotland became James I of England, he decided to unite the two flags. St. George's cross bordered with white, was placed on top of St. Andrew's cross.

This was the first Union Jack which was flown at sea (while on land the separate flags were used).

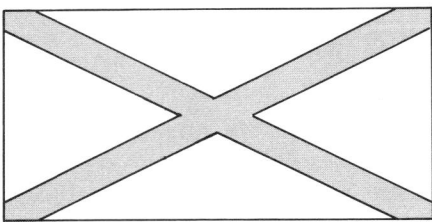

Saint's Day: 17th March
Emblem of Ireland: Shamrock

St. Patrick of Ireland

Nearly two hundred years later in 1801, Ireland was united to England and Scotland. At the time the Irish flag was a gold harp on a blue background. It was decided instead that a red diagonal cross should be placed below the other two. The Scottish flag, being the senior, was given the most important position above the Irish flag in the hoist (nearest flagpole) and below it in the fly (the outer half of the flag).

This is how the present Union Flag was created.

St. David of Wales

Saint's Day: 1st March
Emblem of Wales: Leek

'What about Wales?', you ask. Well, the Welsh flag is not a cross, and therefore cannot be used in the Union Flag.

The flag is a red dragon on a white and green field. Legend has it that Merlin the Wizard saw in a vision a white dragon killing a red dragon. Then a short time later, saw the red dragon come to life. It was thought that this symbolised the failure of the Saxons to conquer Wales.

When a Sixer breaks the flag at the beginning of Pack Meetings or on a new day at camp, we stand smartly at the alert and salute the flag when the Sixer does. At the end of a happy evening when the flag is slowly lowered, we just stand smartly at the alert. We cannot salute a flag that is no longer flying.

Remember, we should always show respect for other countries' flags and National Anthems.

One of the duties of a Sixer is to prepare the flag for breaking. If the flag is to break correctly, it must be folded properly:

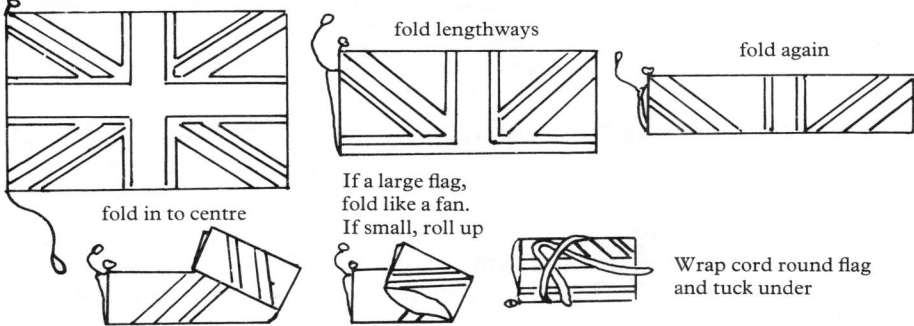

fold in to centre

fold lengthways

fold again

If a large flag, fold like a fan. If small, roll up

Wrap cord round flag and tuck under

Attach toggle to the loop of cord on the flagpole. Join the other two cords with a sheetbend. Hoist flag carefully to the top of the flagpole, with toggle at the top. Secure one cord to hook, and let the cord that is to be pulled hang loose.

Things to Do

● Find out about the national flag and song of another country. Draw and paint the flag, or better still, make one of material for use at an International evening.

- Together with your Six, mime a story about the life of one of our Patron Saints.
- Make up a special prayer for each of the Saint's Days, and read it out at the end of your Pack Meeting.
- Flags have been planted at the top of Everest, at the South Pole and on the Moon. Why not ask Akela if you can have a special Pack Meeting using one of these themes. Each Six could represent a different country, and try to be the first to plant their flag.
- Suppose you have been asked to design a flag for a new city under the sea or maybe on the Moon. What would it look like?
- Join up the correct partners:

Pirates	Yellow
Quarantine	Red
Safety or warning of wreck	White
Danger	Skull and crossbones
Surrender	Black
Mourning	Green

- Two books for your Pack library: 'Flags' by I. O. Evans—a Hamlyn all-colour paperback; 'Ladybird Book of Flags'.

BADGE LINK

Communicator

Discovering

Make and fly a kite

Did you know that kites are one of the oldest toys in the world? Long before balloons or aeroplanes were invented, man used man-lifting kites for a variety of reasons. There are stories of men being carried into cities to spy on the inhabitants, and of kites being used to fly equipment to men trapped on mountains.

The Chinese are famous for their colourful kites which come in all shapes and sizes—huge birds, fierce dragons and brightly coloured fishes. These are used in many of their festivals.

KITE SAFETY CODE
- Never fly a kite near overhead power lines.
- Do not fly a kite near crowds, busy roads or railways.
- It is against the law to fly kites over 60 m or within three miles of any airport.

HOMEMADE KITE

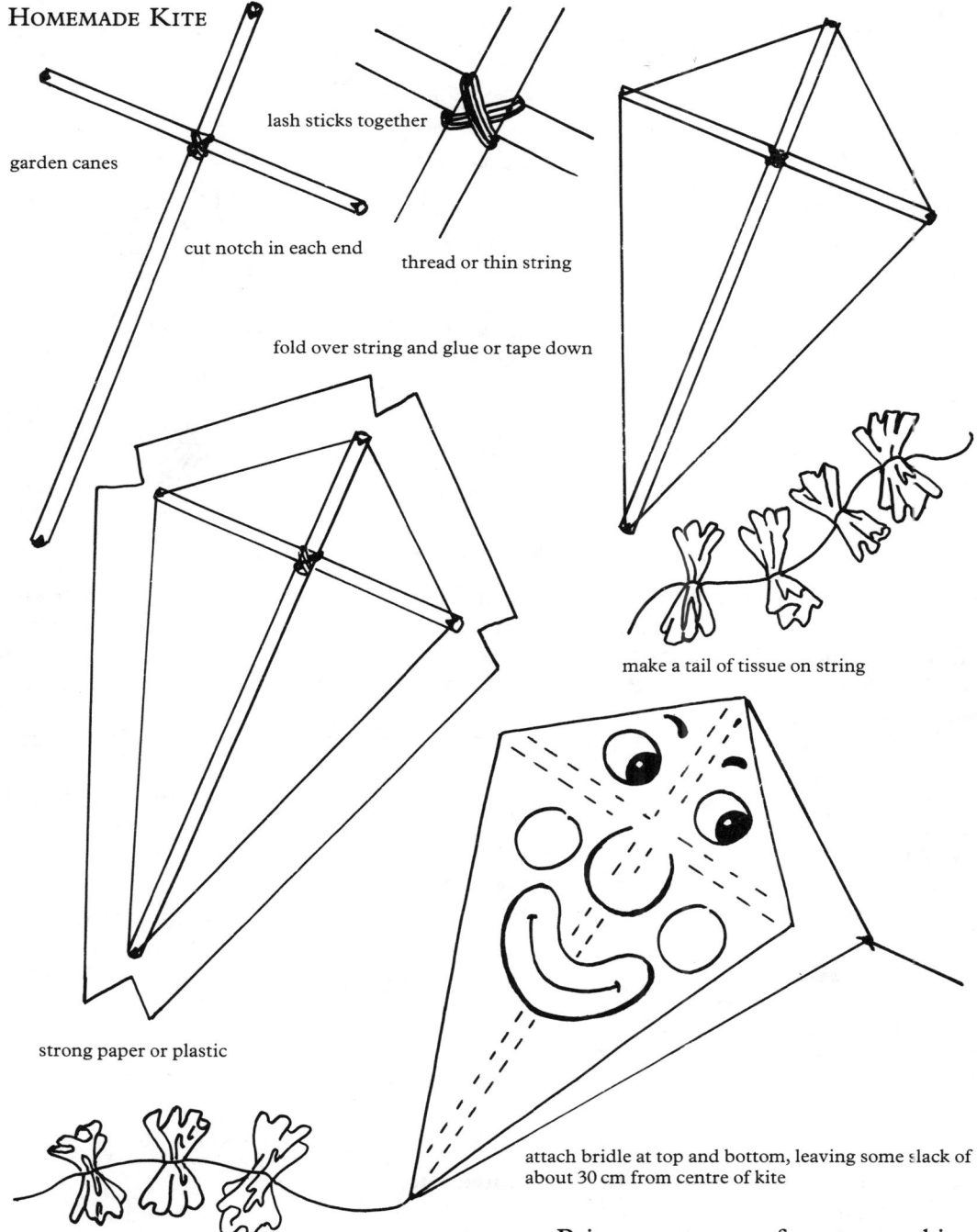

garden canes

lash sticks together

cut notch in each end

thread or thin string

fold over string and glue or tape down

make a tail of tissue on string

strong paper or plastic

attach bridle at top and bottom, leaving some slack of about 30 cm from centre of kite

Paint patterns or a face on your kite.

Now, all you need is a large ball of string.
Wind this on to a thick stick.

If the kite nose dives, adjust the bridle.
Another shape to try:

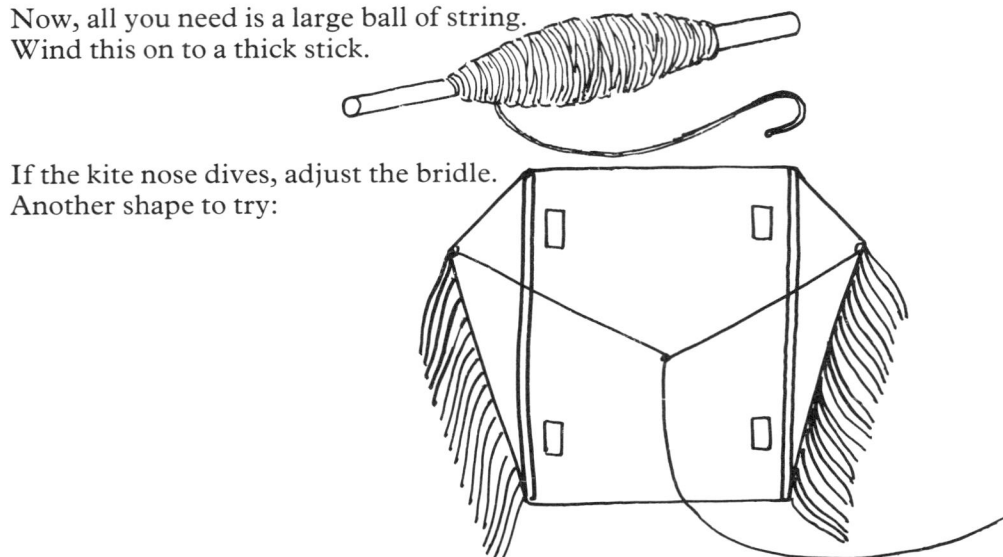

Things to Do

● Kite Festivals are held from time to time in various parts of the country. If one comes your way, make a point of attending. Enthusiasts, both young and old come from miles around to display their creations.

● Ask Akela if the Pack can hold a Father and Son kite making and flying afternoon.

● Try making a kite in the shape of a fish or a dragon. Then find out all you can about Chinese Festivals.

● The Japanese are famous for their miniature kites. Make one from tissue paper and try to fly it.

● Winds of 8–15 miles per hour are ideal for the average kite. Learn more about the Beaufort scale to help you to measure the wind speed.

● Learn the knots useful in kite making:

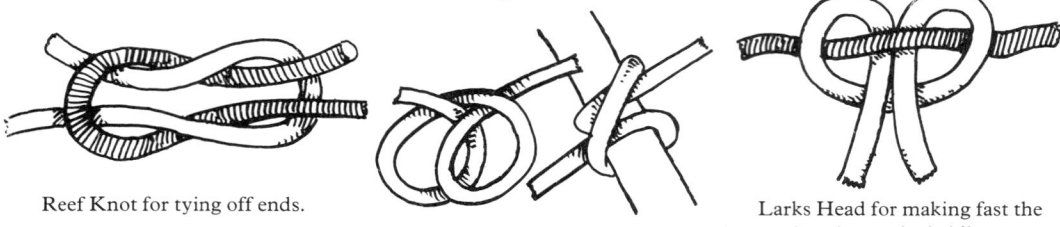

Reef Knot for tying off ends.   Clove Hitch for tying on the bow of the tail.   Larks Head for making fast the towing ring to the bridle.

● Hold a competition for the best decorated kite.

● Read 'Making and Flying Kites' by Lloyd, Mitchell and Thomas and published by Beaver Books. Also 'Kites' by Malcolm McPhun and published by Macdonald.

Discovering

Grow a plant in a garden or a plant pot

Have you ever grown anything?—a plant, a bulb for Christmas flowering or flowers from seeds. Growing things is easy as long as you remember that all plants need warmth, light and water to make them thrive.

You do not need lots of space. If you live in a town you can grow your plants in pots or in window boxes. Some plants grow better in the shade, and others in full sun. Some need plenty of water and others need very little. Ask a keen gardener to advise you or read the instructions carefully on the back of the seed packets.

Why not begin with something simple like mustard and cress? This is one with a crop that you can really eat. Lay some damp kitchen paper on a saucer and sprinkle it with the seed. Mustard seed grows faster than cress, so sow the mustard seeds three days later. Cover the seeds and keep the paper moist. When the seeds start producing shoots, remove the cover.

CARROT PLANT

Just slice off the top and stand the carrot in a saucer with a little water. Keep it in the light.

After a week or two, you will have a very pretty plant.

Try another root crop—a raw beetroot.

CITRUS FRUITS—oranges, lemons and grapefruit

Fill some pots or the skins of the fruit cut in half, with Compost and plant your pips. Keep them well watered and put them in a warm dark place, covered with kitchen paper or foil. They may take one to two months before any shoots appear, so you will need to be patient.

E

BEAN SPROUTS

Why not try growing bean sprouts? There are many types to choose from in your local garden centre. Put a level tablespoon of seed into a clean empty jam jar (the volume of seed will increase by the time it is ready for eating by up to ten times). Cover the jar with a piece of muslin and secure with an elastic band. Fill the jar with tepid water, shake thoroughly and drain. Do this twice and then leave lying on its side anywhere safe. Repeat the process of filling with tepid water and draining twice a day until ready for eating. The packet will tell you how long according to the type of seed. Either eat the beans raw or fry in a pan with perhaps some other vegetables or meat.

BULBS

Look in the shops around September for hyacinth bulbs which have been specially treated so they will bloom at Christmas. Buy some bulb fibre and fill the pot three quarters full. Water well, and then plant the bulbs about one cm deep. Lightly cover the pot and keep in a cool dark place for about two months, and then bring them out into the light.

If you are thinking of growing plants in the garden, the possibilities are endless. Why not try lettuces and radishes. You get results fairly quickly, and again they are plants that you can eat. If you prefer, there are many packets of annual flower seeds to choose from. You will find the instructions for growing both vegetables and flowers on the seed packets.

Things to Do

- Grow bulbs to give to local old folk as a Pack good turn at Christmas.
- Ask Akela if the Pack can hold a 'Potato Growing Competition'. Each Cub is given one seed potato to plant in his garden. At a set time the plant is dug up, and its potatoes are weighed. Why not bag up the potatoes and give them to local old folk?
- Visit a botanical garden to gain ideas.
- Visit a garden centre or shop and look out for the more unusual quick-growing plants such as Chinese Bean Shoots which can be grown in a jam jar.
- Hold a sponsored 'Grow a Sunflower' with so much money for every 30 cm. Give the money to charity.
- Make a miniature garden on a plate or biscuit tin lid. Use moss for lawns and painted fir cones for spruce trees. Paths can be made with Plaster of Paris and made to look like crazy paving, or you can use the gravel that is sold for fish tanks. If you want a pond, use foil or a small mirror. A sundial can be made with a cotton reel and card. Arrange small rock plants and cactus in your garden.
- Pressed flowers and leaves: collect these on a dry sunny day, and press them between the pages of a book. Place the book under a heavy weight. During the autumn or winter, you will be able to make your own birthday cards, bookmarkers, etc. Cover the arrangement with sticky-backed plastic to protect it.

BADGE LINK

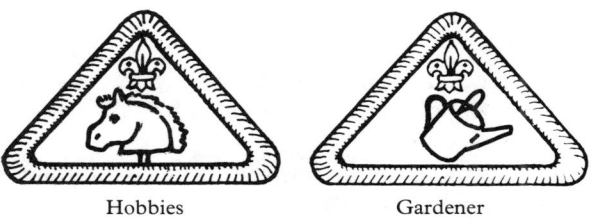

Hobbies   Gardener

Thinking

Find out something about three different forms of communication, such as radio, television, semaphore, smoke signals, drums, newspapers, telephone, etc.

Today there are many ways we can communicate with other people, from simple miming to communications satellites.

It is possible to communicate without any sound. We can frown, smile, show astonishment, nod our heads in agreement and beckon with our hands. Hindu dancers talk with their hands, and the Indians developed a sign language.

The deaf have a sign language of their own.

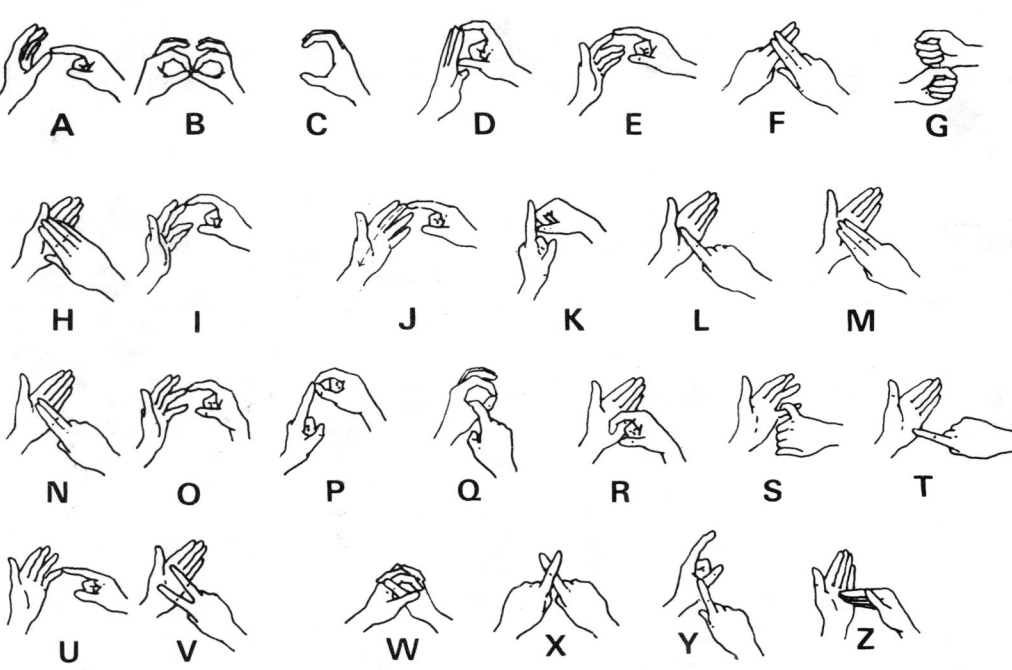

When talking with the deaf: always face them directly; never shout, but speak slowly and clearly; use short sentences.

In Nelson's time, flags were the usual form of signalling from one ship to another. Each signal flag stood for either a number, letter or special instruction.

Do you know what Nelson's famous signal to his fleet was before the Battle of Trafalgar?

Semaphore is fun to learn, and can be used in many of your Pack Wide Games. Why not make your own flags? You will need two sticks about 50 cm long. The flags should be 30 cm square, half blue and half white, as shown in the diagram:

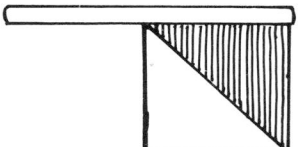

- When you are signalling, always face the person who is receiving your message.
- Stand with your feet about 30 cm apart, and don't wobble!
- Hold the stick near the flag. The stick should be an extension of your arm, with your forefinger lying along the back of the stick.

Here is the way that semaphore signals are sent:

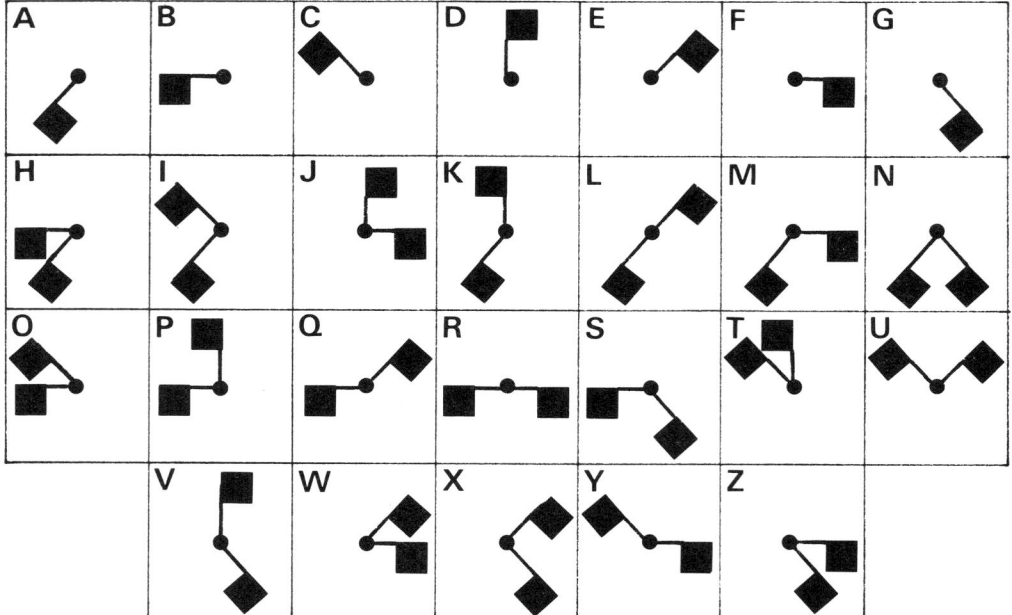

Try learning seven letters at a time, and then see how many words you can make up.

Why not ask Akela to play some taped music like 'Life on the Ocean Wave' to practise to and maybe even put on a display for your parents at the end of a special Navy Evening.

Things to Do

● Make yourself a sailor hat, and perhaps each Six could represent a different ship.
● Find out about the International Code of Signals for Shipping.
● Trafalgar Day is on 21st October—why not make your own ships and organise a battle.

RADIO

Radio is not just the small portable you have in your home. Policemen on patrol carry a two-way radio, the control room at airports and the radio room of a ship are an important and sometimes vital form of communication.

Do you know who constructed the first practical radio?

Things to Do

● Why not get together with your Six, and form your own Broadcasting Company? Tape a fifteen minute programme. It could be all pop, or perhaps local news and weather followed by a Radio Quiz.

MORSE

Morse has many advantages over semaphore, but is perhaps more difficult to learn. Morse code consists of a series of dots and dashes, and can be sent with flags, a torch, signalling lamp or an electric buzzer.

A	● ━		M	━ ━		Y	━ ● ━ ━
B	━ ● ● ●		N	━ ●		Z	━ ━ ● ●
C	━ ● ━ ●		O	━ ━ ━		1	● ━ ━ ━ ━
D	━ ● ●		P	● ━ ━ ●		2	● ● ━ ━ ━
E	●		Q	━ ━ ● ━		3	● ● ● ━ ━
F	● ● ━ ●		R	● ━ ●		4	● ● ● ● ━
G	━ ━ ●		S	● ● ●		5	● ● ● ● ●
H	● ● ● ●		T	━		6	━ ● ● ● ●
I	● ●		U	● ● ━		7	━ ━ ● ● ●
J	● ━ ━ ━		V	● ● ● ━		8	━ ━ ━ ● ●
K	━ ● ━		W	● ━ ━		9	━ ━ ━ ━ ●
L	● ━ ● ●		X	━ ● ● ━		0	━ ━ ━ ━ ━

Things to Do

- Connect up a bulb and battery and make yourself a signalling lamp.
- Instructions on how to do this are in the Ladybird book 'Magnets and Electricity'.
- Do you know who invented the Morse Code?

NEWSPAPERS

The first English newspaper appeared just before the start of the Civil War in 1641. Today there are many types of newspapers catering for people with differing interests.

What newspaper does your family read? Do you only read the cartoons and perhaps just look up the times of your favourite television programmes?

Perhaps Akela will ask you to look for pictures and stories of people who have done their best.

Things to Do

- Read the Ladybird books: 'The Story of Newspapers' and 'The Story of Printing'.
- With your Six, make up one sheet of a newspaper. It might contain a cartoon, a 100-word story, a crossword, local history, weather report, a report of a Cub event, a reported interview with the vicar, etc. Put this sheet together with other Sixes, and you will have your own Pack newspaper. What will you call it?

Thinking

Help to plan and carry out a conservation project

It would be very difficult to suggest a particular conservation project that you could carry out in your area, but here are some ideas you could perhaps follow up.

CONSERVATION IN YOUR GARDEN
- Sow flowers with bright colours and sweet scents to attract butterflies, bees and certain beetles.
- Plant buddleia bushes to attract butterflies.
- Grow sunflowers. Leave the seed for the finches.
- Leave a small patch of nettles for butterflies to breed. Old nettles should be cut down to allow fresh ones to grow. *Never* spray with poison.
- Dead leaves under trees are homes for insects.
- Every garden should have a small wild part.

AIR POLLUTION

The many cars on our roads release sulphur dioxide into our air. This is poisonous to our plants and animals. Do you know which tree stands up to this pollution best and is often seen in the streets of our towns and cities?

Carry out an experiment: Hang some blotting paper on your Mum's clothes' line, and leave it there for one week. What has happened to your blotting paper? (If you live in a rural area, no doubt it will be quite clean.)

WATER POLLUTION

Study a pond or stream in your area: is the pond stagnant, or is it fed by a stream? Do cattle drink here? Would the farmer perhaps allow a small party of Cubs and their Leaders to clean and tidy the area?

Take photographs or make sketches of the pond or stream and surrounding trees and vegetation at various times of the year. Spend an evening pond dipping and make a list of the pond life.

The animals found in a pond or stream are good indicators of the amount of pollution. Some animals can only live in clean water, whilst others can survive in very polluted water. For example, the Mayfly and Stonefly nymph live in clean water, whilst the Freshwater Shrimp can live in slightly polluted water.

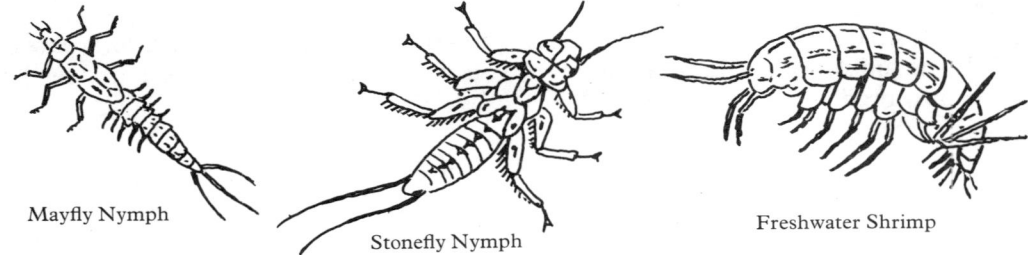

Mayfly Nymph

Stonefly Nymph

Freshwater Shrimp

The Water Louse, Bloodworm and Sludgeworm can live in very polluted water.

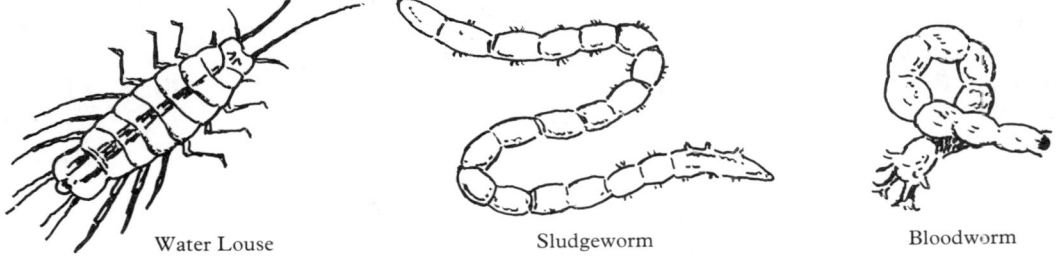

Water Louse

Sludgeworm

Bloodworm

Visit a farm. (Ask Akela to arrange this for you through The National Farmers Union.) Ask the farmer about the farming year, and find out about crop rotation. Have some hedges been removed to make way for bigger machinery?

Try this experiment on your return home: Dig up some soil from your garden and weigh it. Place it on newspaper and leave it for a few days. Now weigh the soil again. What has happened and why? Do you know why earthworms are important to our land?

WHY ARE HEDGES IMPORTANT TO OUR COUNTRYSIDE?

Make a study of a stretch of hedgerow. You will find that it is made up of quite a collection of plants and wildlife. Hawthorn is an important part of a hedge. Not only is it quick growing, but it provides food for many creatures. Some birds will make their nests in a hedge and field mice, shrews, voles and moles may be found there.

Hawthorn

It can be great fun to try and date a hedge: Measure out a 30 m stretch of hedge. Count the shrubs and trees (not the smaller plants). It is thought that one shrub or tree becomes established every hundred years, so if you find a hedge with four different shrubs and trees in it, you can reckon that the hedge is around 400 years old. With the aid of an old large scale map, you will be able to see where hedges have been uprooted.

Things to Do

● If you want to see the development of a caterpillar into a butterfly, you should collect a couple of black caterpillars, usually found on stinging nettles, towards the end of June. Place them in a shoe box with plenty of air holes, and put some transparent plastic over the top. Feed them each day with fresh stinging nettle leaves. In a few weeks they will change into pupae, and two weeks later the butterflies will emerge. Release them near stinging nettles.

● Read the Ladybird Conservation Books: 'Nature's Roundabout'; 'What on Earth are we Doing'; 'Wild Life in Britain'; 'Hedges'.

BADGE LINK

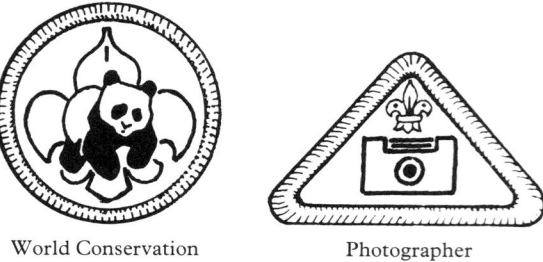

World Conservation   Photographer

Thinking

Help to organise and take part in an act of worship for the Pack

This does not necessarily mean taking part in a church service or a Scouts' Own, but can be taking part in a Biblical story, playing some favourite hymns on your recorder or writing a prayer or story for a special occasion, and then reading it.

Perhaps St. George's Day falls on your Pack Meeting and Akela has asked you to write a special prayer to follow the games and activities connected with this Saint. How would you begin? Well, think about St. George. What words do you associate with him? Perhaps: courage; bravery; good overcoming evil.

> Dear Lord, help us to be like St. George,
> To have the courage to try something new,
> To be brave when faced with danger
> and to know the difference between right and wrong.
>   Amen.

There are many beautiful poems that would fit in with any act of worship—animal poems, story poems and thoughtful poetry.

A lovely story poem entitled 'The Creation'—a Negro sermon in verse, by James Weldon Johnson begins:

> And God stepped out into space,
> And He looked around and said,
> 'I'm lonely—
> I'll make Me a world'

Why not read this and have Gustav Holst's 'The Planets' as background music?

John Masefield's poem 'Roadways' could be read at the end of an evening about the sea.

'The Golden Treasury of Poetry' published by Collins is an excellent book to dip into.

Have you been on holiday and taken some slides that include landscapes, animals, streams, etc.? If Akela has a recording of 'All Things Bright and Beautiful', why not show your slides to this music?

With two other Members of your Six, pretend you are a newspaper reporter, and interview Pilate and Barabbas:

Ask Pilate—

> 'What did you think of Jesus?'
> 'Why did you set Barabbas free?'
> 'How do you feel about it all now?'

Ask Barabbas—

> 'Why were you in prison?'
> 'What sort of punishment were you expecting?'
> 'Did the crowd surprise you when they shouted for *your* release?'

Things to Do

● Visit your place of worship. If this is a parish church, are there any special stories connected with the windows? How old is the font? Why is it always near the entrance of the church? Draw a plan of the building.
● Perhaps you could follow up this visit by making your own stained glass window. Use either black paper with panels cut out and then filled with coloured cellophane or on white paper, colour in a pattern to represent the stained glass, then rub cooking oil carefully over your pattern until it becomes transparent. Hang it up.
● Help to decorate your place of worship for a festival.
● Help to tidy the surrounding area or the building itself.
● Read the Ladybird books: 'What to Look for Inside a Church'; 'What to Look for Outside a Church'. There is also a series of books available through Christian book shops entitled 'Our friends of different faiths'.

Thinking

Find out something about life in your area in the past and act any special events or describe any interesting buildings

Cubs everywhere live in interesting cities, towns and villages. Once you start to explore, you will find out many exciting things about where you live. All you need basically to record the history of your area is a pencil and sketchbook. A camera would add extra interest.

Perhaps the local inn has secret passages used by smugglers, or maybe a famous battle was fought nearby.

Do you know how your town or village got its name, and why it grew up just where it did? If you have a local museum you might find the answer there. A visit to your local library will help you to find out about the history of your area. The librarian will no doubt be able to show you old maps and books. You will not be able to take these away, so you must be prepared to make notes at the library.

The parish church is worth a visit as this may well be the oldest building. As well as a place of worship where people were baptised, married and buried, a church was a meeting place for the local people and a refuge in time of trouble. Look at the brasses. These will give you the names of wealthy people who have lived in your area. Are the descendants of these people still living nearby?

Now, what about the outside of the church? In the churchyard you will find that many of the tombstones make interesting and sometimes sad reading. What is the date of the oldest tombstone? Can you read what is written on it?

Talk to your grandparents or maybe an old person living nearby. They will like to talk about their childhood and how different everything was in their day. Why not use a tape recorder to record your conversation? Maybe Akela will let you play it back at a Pack Meeting.

How many different styles of buildings can you see around you? Are the dates of when they were erected written on them? Notice the chimney pots of the various houses. No doubt you will be surprised at the variety. Chimney pots were used on large houses as long ago as seven hundred years, but it was many centuries later that they were used on small houses. Can you discover how the smoke from fires used to escape out of the houses in those days?

Try to discover how your road got its name. Sometimes roads or squares are named after famous men or women who had some connection with the neighbourhood. You may have a Quebec Square or a Baden-Powell Road. Many roads take their names from some features of the past which have long since disappeared. Barn Avenue was probably part of a farm many years ago, and a road called Ridgeway was possibly named because it was once a straight piece of land bordering a canal or railway.

STREET FURNITURE

Do you know what we mean when we talk about 'street furniture'? It is certainly not tables and chairs, but if you look about you in any busy road, you will see quite an assortment of objects. There might be road signs, bollards, pillar boxes, lamp-posts, coal-hole covers, fire hydrants, traffic lights, bus stops or even a drinking fountain or old well. The latter two are probably no longer used but may be used as a place for plants.

Most of these objects are useful, but what about statues? They have no special use, but were erected to commemorate someone who had contributed something to the area in the past.

Two other relics of the past are a horse trough and a pump. The first supplied drinking water for horses, but fell into disuse when the motor car took over as a means of transport. The second supplied drinking water for the people of a town before the days of piped water.

Things to Do

● From all you have found out, draw a picture of what you think your area must have looked like in the past.

● From the stories you have discovered, make up a play and use puppets to put on a show for a parents' evening.

● Make your own history. For this you will need a small biscuit tin. In it place things like: a picture of the latest fashion in clothes, a toy car, a photograph of yourself, house and school, a daily and local newspaper, favourite ice cream wrapper, an old school exercise book. No doubt you can think of many other things. Dig a fairly deep hole in your garden and bury your carefully sealed biscuit tin. Don't forget to make a note of the exact spot where it is buried.

● Make some rubbings of the coal-hole covers that you may find in the pavements of towns. Many of these have some very attractive patterns and you could build up quite a collection.

BADGE LINK

Photographer   Artist

Thinking

Carry out a survey of boys' clothes, find out what your friends think about them and what they like wearing best

What are your favourite clothes? What do your friends enjoy wearing? Do you have your favourite winter and summer clothes?

Carry out a shoe survey among your family and friends: how many have lace-ups, slip-ons, buckles, etc. Try doing rubbings of soles of shoes. You will end up with quite a variety of patterns.

Find out what Akela wore when he was your age. Carry out a survey among your relations and neighbours. What did your grandfather wear when he was your age, and how does it vary from your clothes today?

Display photographs or do some drawings. Perhaps visit your local library to find a book on children's clothing over the past fifty years.

Help Akela to plan a Pack Meeting 1920s style, and the following week a Pack Meeting for the year 2000. Dress up in the appropriate clothes.

Why stop at a survey of clothing—try these:

COMICS

What comics do you read?
How do these compare with what your friends read?
Which do you consider the best value for money?
Which is the most expensive, cheapest, etc.?
Which is the funniest, the most violent, etc.?

SHOPS IN YOUR TOWN

How many shoe shops, clothes shops or supermarkets are there in your High Street.

List the most expensive goods, the best value for money, the most variety, special offers, etc.

Things to Do

● Ask Akela to arrange a visit behind the scenes of your local supermarket.
● What do the Royal Family wear on the many occasions they are in the public eye on special duties and when they are on holiday? Collect newspaper and magazine pictures and stick them into a small scrapbook.
● Find out how the Cub Scout uniform varies in other countries throughout the world.
● What do Cub Scouts in other countries eat at tea-time? Perhaps each Six could prepare something from a different country and invite another Six to join them for a tea party.

Collector

Sharing

Invent a 'car passenger code' of behaviour and some travel games

How many times have your parents said 'Please stop messing about in the back, I just can't concentrate' or 'Stop kicking the back of my seat. It's irritating.'

Long journeys can be boring, but it is dangerous to distract the driver. Make preparations beforehand.

Ask your parents if you can help to plan the route. Write down all the places you will have to pass through, and tick them off your list as you go along. Make a note of the mileage to each place, and make a guess on how long it will take to reach it.

Take a small bag or box of useful items: pencils, rubber and pencil sharpener; a pad of plain paper; I Spy Books—'I Spy on the Road', 'I Spy in the Street', 'I Spy Car Numbers', 'I Spy on a Car Journey'; paper tissues; packet of barley sugar; map of route. What would you add to this list?

POPULAR CAR GAMES

(*a*) Each person chooses a colour and counts the number of cars of that colour.

(*b*) Make up a word using the letters of car registrations in the same order, i.e. MRG—Margate: LGH—laugh.

(*c*) Choose a make of car, and see who can spot the highest number of their make.

(*d*) Write down the registration letters of the car in front of yours, and look up in the I Spy Book to see where it comes from.

(*e*) Each person makes out a shopping list, i.e. two kippers, six oranges, steak and kidney, a hat, etc. The winner is the first person to spot all the shops he needs.

(*f*) Blind Man's Observation. One person closes his eyes and tries to describe the passing scene, relying entirely on noises heard. Rest act as judges.

JOURNEYS IN THE DARK

Listen to a tape recording of your favourite story.

Telegrams: Choose a word connected with a car, i.e, L A M P S. Now make up a message using each of these letters. You might say 'Lizy ate my pie slowly' or 'Lazy Andrew made Patrick sing'.

Make a list of car games that you can play during the day and also after dark.

What is a Car Code? Well, we have a Water Safety Code for safety in the water, the Highway Code for safety on the road and the Country Code for safety in the country, so a Car Code must be for safety in the car!

Do you wait for the car to stop before getting out? Which door do you use to get out? What must you do before opening the offside door (furthest from the pavement)?

How Can the Following Affect the Driver and
Make a Car Journey Dangerous?

Failure to wear seat belt..
Waving arms out of the windows ....
Shouting and arguing..
Romping about on the back seat ....
Kneeling on the back seat and blocking the back window......................
A pile of articles on the back shelf ....
Playing with torches after dark..
Knees or feet in the back of the driver's seat..................................
Leaning out of the window ....

Things to Do

● Why not compile your own book of car games that your family enjoy most.

● Cub Game: One Cub stands with a mirror. Rest creep towards him. When Cub calls 'stop' all freeze. Boys seen in the mirror are out.

● Try two experiments:

   (*a*) Throw a ball. You will find that at a certain point, your hand stays still, but the ball continues on its way.

   (*b*) Place a small pile of books on the top of your hand. Walk forward quickly and then stop suddenly. You will find that although you stopped, the books continued to move and slid forward.

In a collision between two vehicles, the passengers are frequently injured when they hit the windscreen. An external force stops the car, but the passengers continue their forward motion in accordance with Newton's first law.

The Law says that you must ALWAYS WEAR YOUR SEAT BELT.

Badge Link

Cyclist

Sharing

Make your own weather station with at least two instruments. Keep a log over a period of a fortnight (charts, comments, drawings, etc.).

British people seem obsessed with the weather. We listen avidly to local forecasts and conversations always bring in the weather. Perhaps it is because in Britain our weather is so varied—it's never the same from one week to the next.

How many industries can you think of that are affected by the weather? Well, there is agriculture. Farmers cannot sow their corn or grass seed if we have had a great deal of rain, because the tractors make a mess of the fields. Equally, the corn and grass if sown, will not grow if we have no rain. What about aircraft, shipping and trains? What type of weather disrupts these?

If you wish to study the weather, you can do this by observing daily the air pressure, temperature, wind speed and direction, the clouds and the rainfall.

BEAUFORT SCALE

In 1806, a British Admiral, Sir Francis Beaufort devised a scale for measuring the speed of the wind at sea. It was later adapted for use on land. This is not as accurate a measure as an anemometer, but is still used by people recording weather situations.

Make your own chart like the one below and hang it near your weather station:

Beaufort No.	Wind	Effect	Speed
0	Calm	Smoke rises vertically.	less than 1
1	Light air	Smoke drifts. Wind vanes do not move.	2–5 k.p.h.
2	Light breeze	Leaves rustle. Wind vanes move.	6–11 k.p.h.
3	Gentle breeze	Leaves and small twigs move.	12–19 k.p.h.
$4\frac{1}{2}$	Moderate breeze	Dust raised and paper flutters.	20–29 k.p.h.
5	Fresh breeze	Small trees sway.	30–39 k.p.h.
6	Strong breeze	Large branches move. Umbrellas difficult to use.	40–50 k.p.h.
7	Moderate gale	Whole trees sway.	51–61 k.p.h.
8	Fresh gale	Difficult to walk. Twigs break off trees.	62–74 k.p.h.
9	Strong gale	Damage to roof and chimney pots.	75–87 k.p.h.
10	Whole gale	Trees uprooted.	88–102 k.p.h.

WIND SPEED

To determine the wind speed in miles per hour with a homemade anemometer, you should count the number of revolutions in 30 seconds and then divide by five.

Cut the ends off plastic washing-up bottles.
Colour one of the cups a bright red to make counting easier.

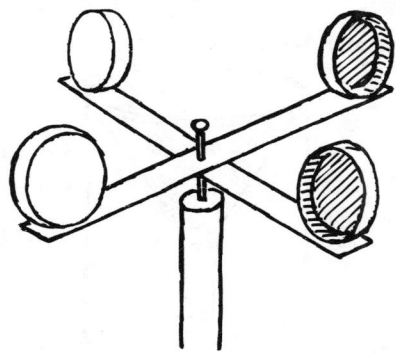

WIND DIRECTION

Small airfields still use wind socks to let the pilot know from which direction the wind is blowing.

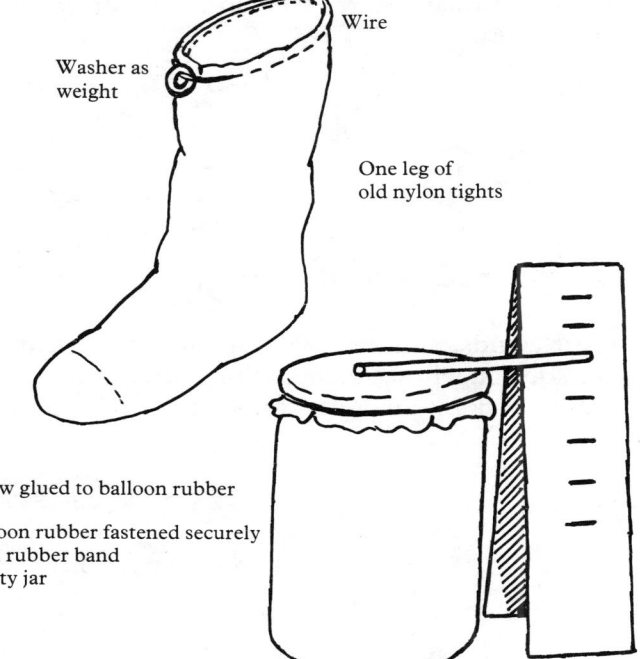

Wire

Washer as
weight

One leg of
old nylon tights

BAROMETER

Straw glued to balloon rubber

Balloon rubber fastened securely
with rubber band
empty jar

F

As the air pressure increases, the rubber pushes down into the jar and the straw rises at the far end. This means the approach of fair weather. When bad weather is approaching, the pressure is less, and the straw will fall.

Find out the air pressure from the daily newspaper, and use this as a starting point for your barometer. Remember to keep your barometer where the temperature is fairly constant.

RAIN GAUGE TO MEASURE AMOUNT OF RAINFALL

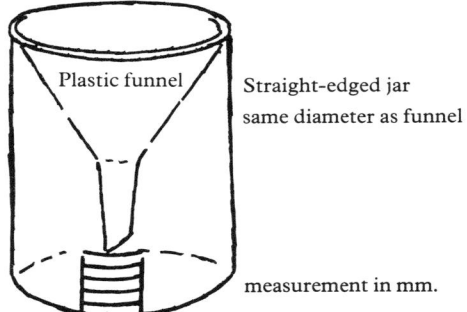

Plastic funnel

Straight-edged jar
same diameter as funnel

measurement in mm.

CLOUDS

There are many different types of clouds, and these can tell you a great deal about the weather once you have learnt to read them correctly. We can split the clouds into three main types:

Cirrus (symbol *ci*)   above 4,500 m

These are the highest clouds, and are made up almost exclusively of ice crystals because they are so cold. You will see them as thin wispy clouds. They usually mean fine weather if the tails are pointing downwards, and rain is approaching if the tails are pointing upwards.

Cumulus (symbol *cu*)   Base of cloud 1,500 m
top may reach 12,000 m

These clouds look rather like cauliflowers. Small Cumulus clouds mean fine weather, but larger clouds can produce showers.

Stratus (symbol *st*)

will sometimes descend to within a few hundred feet of ground level

These layer clouds are the lowest in the sky usually covering hilltops. In winter, these clouds usually indicate drizzle.

You should record on your weather chart each day the state of the sky. For this you will want to use the correct symbols. These are:

b   blue sky (not more than a quarter covered by cloud)
bc   sky partly cloudy (about a half covered)
c   generally cloudy
o   overcast sky
u   threatening sky

RECORDING YOUR OBSERVATIONS

Remember to make your recordings at the same time each day in order to get an accurate comparison.

DATE	Wind direction	Wind speed	Max. temp.	Min. temp.	State of sky	Cloud	Air pressure	Rainfall	Comments
3/5/79	W	3	16°C	9°C	o	St	1023·5	2 m	Dull day
4/5	SW	4	20°C	10°C	bc	Cu	1029	Nil	Brighter

F*

Things to Do

● Make a collection of weather sayings and rhymes. From your own observations, how true are these?

> Cows all lie down when it is going to rain.
> Mackerel sky, mackerel sky, not long wet and not long dry.
> Rain before seven, fine before eleven.
> Oak before the ash, we are in for a splash.
> Ash before the oak we'll surely have a soak.

MAKE A WEATHER POSTER

Use cotton wool for Cumulus. Add black felt tip for Cumulonimbus the thunder cloud; thin wisps of cotton wool for Cirrus; tissue paper for Stratus.

MAKE A WEATHER MAN

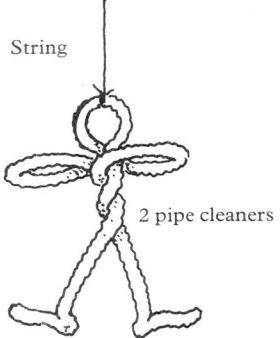

String

2 pipe cleaners

Twist the pipe cleaners into a man, and dip him into a solution of cobalt chloride. Hang him outside. In damp weather he will be pink, but in dry weather he will turn blue.

Collect weather forecast and maps each day from your daily newspaper. Compare this forecast with your own.

Look in your local telephone directory for numbers to dial for forecasts in all parts of Britain.

If you have a camera, take photographs of the various cloud types.

An experiment: Put the same amount of water in a tall jar and a saucer. Which evaporates quicker? Why do you think this is so?

BADGE LINK

Scientist   Photographer

Sharing

On a Pack outdoor activity show that you know the Country Code and the reasons for it

1. ENJOY THE COUNTRYSIDE AND RESPECT ITS LIFE AND WORK

Try to set a good example when in the countryside. Learn to understand the way of life and the work that goes on in the countryside.

2. GUARD AGAINST ALL RISKS OF FIRE

During a dry spell, the danger of fire is very great. The causes are usually matches or cigarette ends thrown carelessly away while still alight. Fires cause devastation of acres of woodland or moorland, and kill wild life.

NEVER LIGHT A FIRE ANYWHERE WITHOUT PERMISSION.

3. FASTEN ALL GATES

If you have to open a gate when out on an expedition, make sure it is safely closed behind you. A gate left open means animals will wander, maybe into traffic or perhaps into a neighbouring field where they might gorge themselves to death.

If you cannot open a gate, and have to climb over, always make sure you climb over at the hinged end so as not to spoil the hang of the gate.

If you find a gate open on farmland, leave it. That entrance may be the animals' only access to water.

4. KEEP YOUR DOGS UNDER CLOSE CONTROL

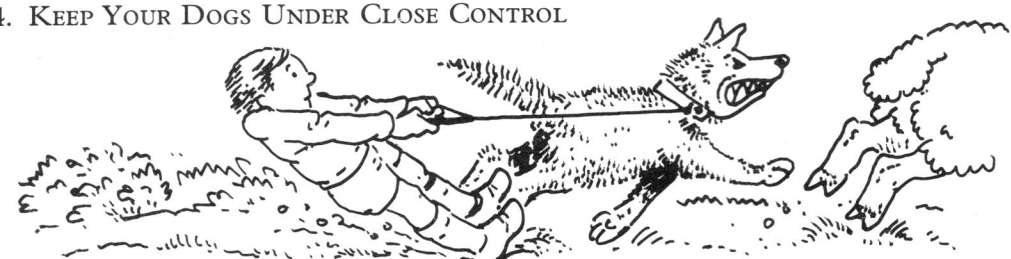

Keep your dog on a lead when there is livestock about. A dog allowed to run loose among cows causing them to panic, can make the milk yield drop, or a dog chasing sheep can cause heavy losses of lambs in the spring time.

Farmers will shoot any dog found worrying livestock, and its owner may have to pay heavy compensation.

Always keep your dog on a lead on country roads.

5. KEEP TO PUBLIC PATHS ACROSS FARM LAND

Crops can be ruined by people walking over them. Remember too that grass is a very valuable crop to a farmer. Although the long grass may look inviting for a picnic or to play in, once flattened, it is very difficult to harvest for hay or silage.

When a path crosses a field or goes round the edge of one, always walk in single file.

6. USE GATES AND STILES TO CROSS FENCES, HEDGES AND WALLS

Do not climb over walls or through hedges. They are very expensive items to repair, and if damaged can mean that livestock will escape.

Always keep to the paths and use the styles or gates.

7. LEAVE LIVESTOCK, CROPS AND MACHINERY ALONE

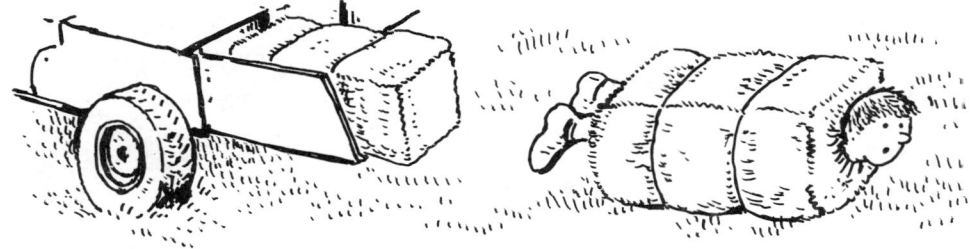

Keep well away from working machinery. If you stand behind a large tractor or trailer, the farmer will not be able to see you. These days, a busy farmyard is a very dangerous place to be. Farm machinery is often left out-of-doors unprotected, and bales of hay or straw might be piled up in the fields. Never play amongst them.

8. TAKE YOUR LITTER HOME

All litter is unsightly and is difficult to dispose of in the country. It is also dangerous. Broken bottles can cut an animal's foot. Plastic bags left lying about never disintegrate naturally and can kill a sheep or cow if they eat them.

Always take a spare bag with you to collect all your rubbish in. Then take it home.

9. HELP TO KEEP ALL WATER CLEAN

Never wash in or foul fresh water, and never interfere with any of the cattle troughs you may come across on your walks, as water is vital to livestock.

10. PROTECT WILDLIFE, PLANTS AND TREES

Do not pick or uproot flowers. Let them remain for other people to enjoy. Do not disturb the wild animals or birds. It only makes their survival a little harder.

Never remove the bark from trees or carve your name on the trunks. Always ask the landowner's permission before cutting sticks from trees for cooking your sausages or twists.

11. TAKE SPECIAL CARE ON COUNTRY ROADS

Country roads present many problems: blind corners, high banks and hedges which conceal people from traffic. There is often mud on the roads caused by slow moving tractors and trailers, or cattle being moved to another field. Remember always to walk facing the oncoming traffic.

If you are in a car with your parents, ask them to avoid parking in front of a field gate or farm entrance.

12. MAKE NO UNNECESSARY NOISE

Remember that sounds travel; keep your portable radio down low. Instead, enjoy the natural sounds around you.

Things to Do

● Make a poster of one of the above Country Code rules. Maybe each Six could make a poster on the various rules. Perhaps Akela will arrange for them to be displayed in a shop window.
● Have you a camera? If so, perhaps you could take photographs representing the 12 parts of the Country Code. The rest of your Six could help by working out each part.
● With your Six, mime one part of the Country Code. See if the rest of the Pack can guess which one it is.
● Draw a picture on postcards to represent each of the 12 rules. Write out the rules on separate postcards, and then try matching the picture to the rule.
● Go on a footpath survey with some other Cubs and Akela. Make a note of the types of trees and wild flowers. Describe the walk, i.e. direction, length, various views, etc. Perhaps you could compile your own Pack local footpath guide.

LINK WITH OTHER ARROW ACTIVITIES

Sharing: Go on an expedition to a farm, and discuss how it helps the community.

Sharing: Do three different jobs for a farmer.

Discovering: Watch three different types of machinery at work.

BADGE LINK

World Conservation Badge

Explorer

Photographer

Sharing

Visit a railway station or bus station and learn how to use a timetable

If you have helped to plan an expedition by train or bus, you will have noticed that the timetables use the 24 hour clock system. The armed forces and many European countries use this system in order to avoid the confusion of the A.M. and P.M. system.

Instead of dividing the day into two twelve hour periods with the first twelve hours called A.M. (this comes from the Latin *Ante meridiem* which means BEFORE noon) and the next twelve hours called P.M. (this comes from the Latin *Post meridiem* which means afternoon), the 24 hour clock system uses the twenty-four hours for each day and calls them 1 to 24 hours, although midnight is always written 00.00.

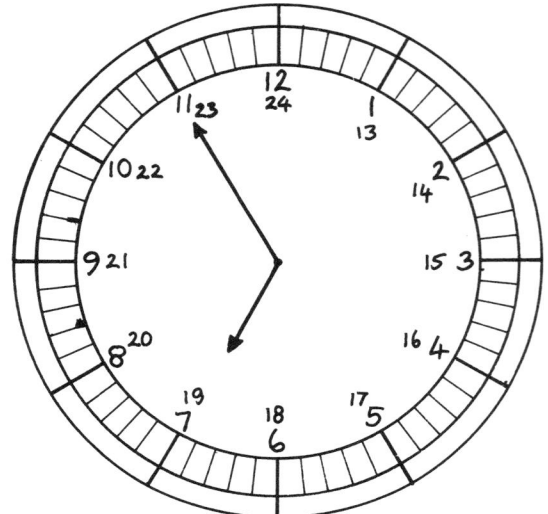

Two o'clock in the morning is written 02.00, and we say '0-two hundred hours'. Fifteen minutes past six in the morning is written 06.15, and we say '0-six fifteen hours'.

Four o'clock in the afternoon is 16.00 hours. This is because it is sixteen hours since the day began at midnight.

The first two numbers show the hours, and the last two the minutes.

See if you can fill in the gaps:

A.M. and P.M. Clock	24 hour Clock
1 A.M.	
	19.07 hours
4.30 P.M.	
half past eight in the morning	
	21.35 hours
2.30 P.M.	

Things to Do

● Make a World Clock: With this you will be able to tell what time it is in different countries of the World.

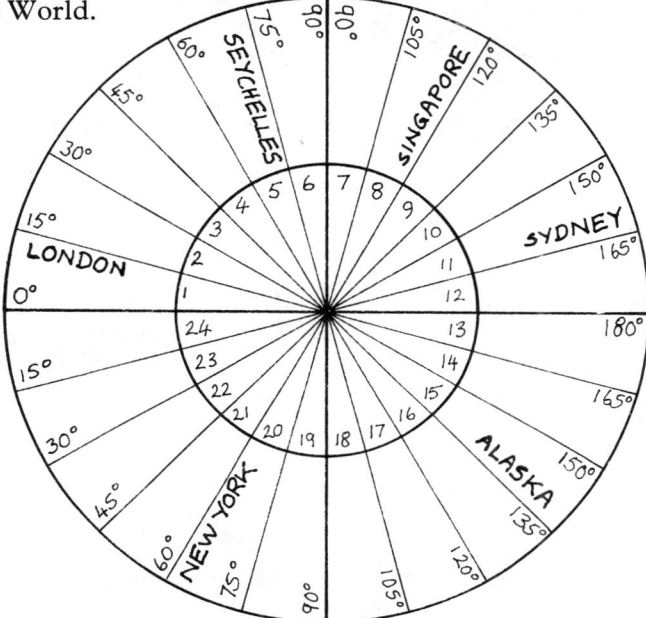

Make two circles of card with the words and number in the above diagram written on, and fasten the smaller to the larger one so that the smaller one rotates. Use a globe or atlas to help you to fill in the blank spaces.

If you were to travel across America, you would find the time changes by one hour at certain places. This happens when you enter new time zones. If you look at a globe or atlas you will see lines called meridians that go from pole to pole. These meridians are 15 degrees apart.

● Decide where to visit. Look at the timetable to see when the train or bus leaves and its arrival at your destination. Check on the time of the return transport, and find out the cost.

Or better still: Make your own travel brochure to a place of your choice. Show the route, plus interesting places that are passed on the way. Paint your own pictures or use postcards. Give details of rail or bus times and include the cost. List places of interest in and around your chosen place.

TAKE AKELA AND THE REST OF YOUR SIX TO THE PLACE YOU HAVE CHOSEN.

● Make your own Sun Clock: Choose a sunny position. Knock a short stick into the ground and draw a circle round it. Mark the circle with a stone where the shadow falls at the end of each hour. Are the stones equally spaced?

Look at your clock a few weeks later. What has happened?

● Read 'The How and Why Wonder Book of Time'—Transworld Publishers.

Badge Link

Explorer Badge   Map Reader

Sharing

Using a map, help to plan a route for your summer holiday or a Pack expedition

First choose the most suitable map for your holiday or Pack expedition: 'The Ordnance Survey Route Planning Map of Great Britain'. This is used for advance planning of long distance motoring. The scale is 1 cm to 6·25 km.

The primary routes are in green.

Large towns are marked round in yellow.

'The Routemaster Series of Great Britain' is also for car journeys, and shows both fast direct routes as well as the more pleasant cross-country roads. The scale is 1 cm to 2·5 km.

The 1.50 000 map series is the one most people use and is suitable for expeditions on foot, by bicycle or by car. The scale is 2 cm to 1 km. These maps show parking places, footpaths, National Trust properties, bus and coach stations, etc. If you need greater detail, then the 1.25 000 scale maps are for you. The scale is 4 cm to 1 km.

If you use one of the 1.50 000 maps, you will need to know the meanings of the various map symbols. Symbols depicting important buildings are shown on maps with initial letters or abbreviations:

PH	public house
Sch	school
Hosp	hospital
P	post office
T	telephone

There are symbols for roads showing whether they are minor or major roads. There are also symbols for railway lines, power lines, bus stations, rivers, bridges or marshy ground:

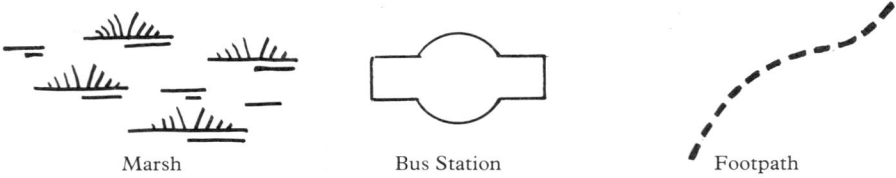

Marsh   Bus Station   Footpath

There are symbols for landmarks such as a church or windmill:

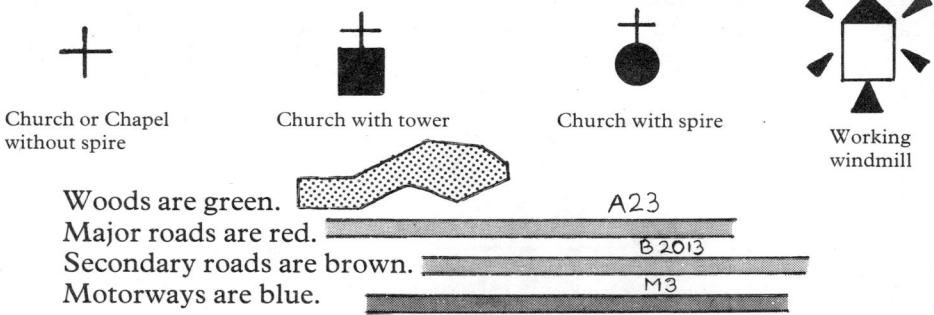

Church or Chapel   Church with tower   Church with spire
without spire   Working
                                                                         windmill

Woods are green.
Major roads are red.   A23
Secondary roads are brown.   B 2013
Motorways are blue.   M3

When planning a journey, whether by car or on foot, it is important to understand about contour lines. Each contour line shows all places which are a certain height above sea level. Contour lines drawn on a map will tell you whether the land is flat or hilly. They will also tell you how steep the hills are, because the closer together the lines, the steeper the hill. If you want to find out more about contour lines, why not ask your teacher?

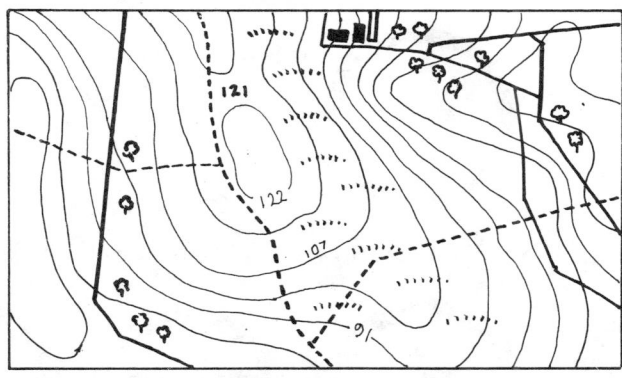

Things to Do

● Make your own map cards, about 9 cm square, in sets of three, i.e.

Draw the symbol on one, what it stands for on another and then try to obtain a picture postcard or photograph showing the correct building or place cut to size for the third card.

Do this with several symbols and then challenge your friends to match them up.

● If you want to measure the number of miles you will have to travel to your journey's end, use a thin piece of string and lay it along the roads you will take. Measure this along the scale at the side of your map.

● Read 'Maps and Map Games' by Deborah Manley and published by Piccolo.

BADGE LINK

Map Reader

Sharing

Draw five traffic signs or symbols and know what they mean

Did you know that there are FOUR different types of road signs? There are the signs that give orders—mostly red circles.

 this means YOU MUST NOT

What you MUST NOT DO is shown inside each circle:

no cycling   no pedestrians   no overtaking   no right turn

 this means YOU MUST

What you MUST DO is shown inside each circle:

Route to be used by pedal cyclists only   ahead only   turn left ahead   mini-roundabout

There are the signs that give warnings of danger ahead—the red triangles;

   This means danger ahead

The danger is shown inside each triangle:

traffic merges from left   two-way traffic crosses one-way road   roundabout   Road narrows on both sides

There are the signs giving INFORMATION:

No through road   Hospital ahead   Parking place

Finally there are the signs giving DIRECTION:

Holiday route

The road marking that goes with this sign

is:

If the sign is hidden by a tree or hedge, you still have the road markings. Equally, if snow covers the road marking, you have a clear sign.

Discover for yourself the road marking that goes with this sign:

Things to Do

● Go for a walk with a friend and look for traffic signs. Do you think they are in a good position? Can you see any places where you think signs ought to be, but are not at present?

● Road signs are the language of our roads. Can you make a list of signs used in other situations?

For example: Scouts and Cub Scouts lay tracking signs;

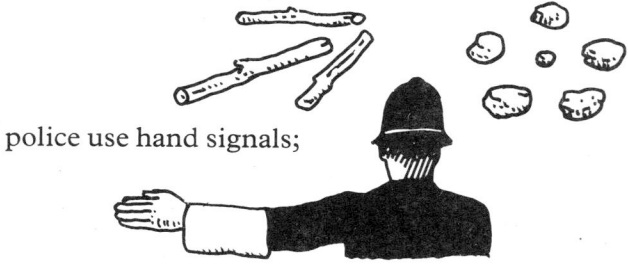

police use hand signals;

a motorist signals.

I am moving out to the right or turning right

- Make up your own sign for 'A Cub Scout Meeting in process'.
- What do these traffic signs indicate? (Tick the correct answer.)

two hump-back bridges
uneven road
wall ahead

no entry
turn ahead
no U turns

two-way traffic crosses
a one-way road
go either way
keep to own side

parachute dropping area
rain—slippery road
hazard

do not drink and drive
slippery road
change lanes

no overtaking
no parking
no motor vehicles

BADGE LINK

Cyclist